Developing Questions
for Focus Groups

Richard A. Krueger

Developing Questions for Focus Groups

Focus Group Kit 3

SAGE Publications
International Educational and Professional Publisher
Thousand Oaks   London   New Delhi

For information:

 SAGE Publications, Inc.
2455 Teller Road
Thousand Oaks, California 91320
E-mail: order@sagepub.com

SAGE Publications Ltd.
6 Bonhill Street
London EC2A 4PU
United Kingdom

SAGE Publications India Pvt. Ltd.
M-32 Market
Greater Kailash I
New Delhi 110 048 India

Printed in the United States of America

Library of Congress Cataloging-in-Publication Data

Morgan, David L., Krueger, Richard A.
  The focus group kit.
    p. cm.
  Includes bibliographical references and indexes.
  Contents: v. 1. The focus group guidebook/David L. Morgan. v. 2. Planning focus groups/David L. Morgan. v. 3. Developing questions for focus groups/Richard A. Krueger. v. 4. Moderating focus groups/Richard A. Krueger. v. 5. Involving community members in focus groups/Richard A. Krueger, Jean A. King. v. 6. Analyzing and reporting focus group results/Richard A. Krueger.

ISBN 0-7619-0760 (pbk.: The focus group kit: alk. paper)

1. Focus groups. I. Title. II. Series. III. Morgan, David L. IV. Krueger, Richard A.

H61.28K778 1997
001.4'33—dc21   97-21135

ISBN 0-7619-0818-8 (v. 1 pbk.)
ISBN 0-7619-0817-X (v. 2 pbk.)
ISBN 0-7619-0819-6 (v. 3 pbk.)
ISBN 0-7619-0821-8 (v. 4 pbk.)
ISBN 0-7619-0820-X (v. 5 pbk.)
ISBN 0-7619-0816-1 (v. 6 pbk.)

This book is printed on acid-free paper.

98 99 00 01 02 03 10 9 8 7 6 5 4 3 2 1

Acquiring Editor:	Marquita Flemming
Editorial Assistant:	Frances Borghi
Production Editor:	Diana E. Axelsen
Production Assistant:	Karen Wiley
Typesetter/Designer:	Janelle LeMaster
Cover Designer:	Ravi Balasuriya
Cover Illustration:	Anahid Moradkhan
Print Buyer:	Anna Chin

Brief Table
of Contents

Detailed Table
of Contents

Acknowledgments

I 've always been impressed with the power of a good question. A good question tests our assumptions, leads us into new area of thinking, and helps us understand ourselves. I've seen the dramatic effect that questions can have. These questions can open the hearts of people, obtain insights as to the logic and views of others, and create reflective thinking. These questions are an essential element of the focus group interview. Effective questions allow participants to ponder the topic and respond from their personal reality.

Thanks to Robert Merton and his colleagues for first introducing the disciplined strategy that has become known as focus group interviewing. Many others have assisted in perfecting the art of asking truly effective questions. Hundreds of professional moderators over the past five decades have created strategies and protocols for focus group questions. These professional moderators, particularly those of the Qualitative Research Consultants Association (QRCA), willingly shared their ideas and approaches to asking truly effective questions.

David Morgan, friend and valued colleague, invited me to assist in the preparation of books and has offered invaluable suggestions and strategies that clarified the writing and presentation of ideas. Mary Anne Casey carefully read each of the earlier drafts, sharpened the thoughts, and perfected the language. She provided continual encouragement and wise advice on the flow of ideas.

When it comes to asking questions, we have much to learn from children. Children have an openness, an innocence, and a special talent for asking questions. To them, there is no such thing as a foolish question—this is an unfortunate adult creation. Along the way, many children have taught me about asking questions, This past year, I've had an opportunity to listen to the questions of Mary Ann (age 9), Sarah (age 6), and Claire (age 3). I only wish my answers were as good as their questions.

Finally, I wish to acknowledge the contributions of many organizations as they tried new approaches, suggested alternatives, and freely offered their feedback and suggestions. They thought that I was the teacher, but in reality, I was their student.

The production quality was improved by Susan Wladaver-Morgan, who offered editing suggestions. The staff at Sage Publications were most helpful. Their editors were encouraging, creative, and willing to take risks. Special thanks to Diana Axelsen, Ravi Balasuriya, Marquita Flemming, and C. Deborah Laughton for eagerly contributing their talents.

A good book is one that touches us in several ways. It should be serious, yet funny; challenging, yet comfortable. It should raise the level of thought. But most of all, it should be fun to read. The best test is if you read more than what you intended. I hope that this book does that for you. May you find the insight, the seriousness, the guiding principles, and the humor in this volume.

Introduction to the Focus Group Kit

We welcome you to this series of books on focus group interviewing. We hope that you find this series helpful. In this section we would like to tell you a bit about our past work with focus groups, the factors that led to the creation of this series, and an overview of how the book is organized.

We began our studies of focus group interviewing about the same time. Our academic backgrounds were different (David in sociology and Richard in program evaluation), and yet we were both drawn to focus group interviewing in the 1980s. We both had books published in 1988 on focus group interviewing that resulted from our research and practice with the methodology. At that time, we were unaware of one another's work and were pleased to begin a collegial relationship. Over the years, we've continued our studies independently, and occasionally our paths crossed and we had an opportunity to work together. In the last decade, we've worked together in writing articles, sharing advice on research studies, and teaching classes. We have generally found that we shared many common thoughts and concerns about focus group interviewing.

During the 1990s, we found that interest in focus groups continued, and we both prepared second editions for our 1988 books. In 1995, the staff at Sage Publications asked us to consider developing a more in-depth treatment of focus group interviewing that would allow for more detail and guide researchers beyond the basic issues. We pondered the request and thought about how the materials might be presented. We weighed a variety of options and finally developed the kit in its present form. We developed this kit in an effort to help guide both novices and experts.

In these books, the authors have occasionally chosen to use the word *we*. Although the authors share many common experiences with focus groups, our approaches can and do vary, as we hope is the case with other researchers as well. When you see the word *we* in the books of this series, it typically refers to a judgment decision by the specific author(s) of that particular volume. Much of what the authors have learned about focus groups has been acquired, absorbed, and assimilated from the experiences of others. We use *we* in circumstances where one of us personally has experienced a situation that has been verified by another researcher or when a practice or behavior has become standard accepted practice by a body of focus group moderators. The use of *I,* on the other hand, tends to refer to situations and experiences that one of us has witnessed that may not have been verified by other researchers.

In terms of content, we decided on six volumes, each representing a separate theme. The volumes include the following:

- **Volume 1:** *The Focus Group Guidebook*

This volume provides a general introduction to focus group research. The central topics are the appropriate reasons for using focus groups and what you can expect to accomplish with them. This book is intended to help those who are new to focus groups.

- **Volume 2:** *Planning Focus Groups*

This volume covers the wide range of practical tasks that need to get done in the course of a research project using focus groups. A major topic is making the basic decisions about the group's format, such as the size of the groups, their composition, and the total number of groups.

- **Volume 3:** *Developing Questions for Focus Groups*

This book describes a practical process for identifying powerful themes and then offers an easy-to-understand strategy for translating those themes into questions. This book helps make the process of developing good questions doable by outlining a process and offering lots of examples.

- **Volume 4:** *Moderating Focus Groups*

The book is an overview of critical skills needed by moderators, the various approaches that successful moderators use, and strategies for handling difficult situations. Rookie moderators will find this book to be an invaluable guide, and veteran moderators will discover tips and strategies for honing their skills.

- **Volume 5:** *Involving Community Members in Focus Groups*

This book is intended for those who want to teach others to conduct focus group interviews, particularly nonresearchers in communities. Volunteers can often gather and present results more effectively than professionals. A critical element is how the volunteers are trained and the manner in which they work together.

- **Volume 6:** *Analyzing and Reporting Focus Group Results*

Analysis of focus group data is different from analysis of data collected through other qualitative methodologies, and this presents new challenges to researchers. This book offers an overview of important principles guiding focus group research and then suggests a systematic and verifiable analysis strategy.

Early on, we struggled with how these materials might be presented. In order to help you find your way around the series, we developed several strategies. First, we are providing an expanded table of contents and an overview of topics at the beginning of each chapter. These elements help the reader quickly grasp the overall picture and understand the relationship between specific sections. Second, we've attempted to make the indexes as useful as possible. Volumes 2-6 contain two indexes: an index for that volume and a series index to help you find your way around the entire kit of six books. Finally, we are using icons to identify materials of interest. These icons serve several purposes. Some icons help you locate other materials within the series that amplify a particular topic. Other icons expand on a particular point, share a story or tip, or provide background material not included in the text. We like the icons because they have allowed us to expand on certain points without interrupting the flow of the discussion. The icons have also allowed us to incorporate the wisdom of other focus group experts. We hope you find them beneficial. We've also included icons in the book to help you discover points of interest.

The **BACKGROUND** icon identifies the bigger picture and places the current discussion into a broader context.

The **CAUTION** icon highlights an area where you should be careful. These are especially intended to help beginners spot potholes or potential roadblocks.

The **CHECKLIST** icon identifies a list of items that are good to think about; they may or may not be in a sequence.

The **EXAMPLE** icon highlights stories and illustrations of general principles.

The **EXERCISE** icon suggests something you could do to practice and improve your skills, or something you could suggest to others to help them improve their skills.

The **GO TO** icon is a reference to a specific place in this book or one of the other volumes where you will find additional discussion of the topic.

The **KEY POINT** icon identifies the most important things in each section. Readers should pay attention to these when skimming a section for the first time or reviewing it later.

The **TIP** icon highlights a good practice to follow or an approach that has worked successfully for us.

We hope you find this series helpful and interesting.

—Richard A. Krueger
St. Paul, Minnesota

—David L. Morgan
Portland, Oregon

About This Book

We've prepared this book to raise the quality of focus group research, specifically the art of asking questions. Clear and thoughtful questions are a foundation of high-quality focus group research. About a dozen or so questions are asked during a two-hour discussion, and although these questions seem spontaneous, they are the result of considerable thought and effort.

We wrote this book as if we were providing help to a friend. When we offer advice to friends on conducting focus groups, we get straight to the point, avoid unnecessary steps, and, above all, try to help them be successful. We try to do that here. We've also tried to make the book easy to read, easy for finding information quickly, and organized in a way that flows. We've included some tips and suggestions from other moderators that we feel are worth considering. Our only regret is that we didn't include enough humor. Try as we might, developing questions just isn't very funny. However, if you hear of a humorous story that illustrates a point included in this book, let us know, and maybe we can include it in the next edition.

We've assumed that you will be selective with this book. We don't expect that you will read it cover to cover; however, there could be value in doing so. Most researchers, we've found, are selective in their reading, moving back and forth from one chapter to another and using examples and concepts as needed.

This book is presented in three parts. Part I is intended as background about the questioning process. The foundational concepts presented here help readers to anchor their activities on areas of greatest importance, point out basic options on question style, and suggest a process of developing the questions. Part II gives advice on actually writing a questioning route. It is an overview of the mechanics of asking quality questions. This section gives advice on categories of questions, phrasing and sequencing the questions, the use of probes and follow-up questions, and the importance of consistency in questions. Suggestions on pilot testing are also discussed. Finally, in Part III, the reader will find an overview of questions to get participants actively engaged in a focus group discussion.

Part I

Thinking About Questions

Before actually writing the questions for a focus group interview, the researcher should consider several principles that have guided master moderators. These principles are the cornerstone of quality questions. Once these principles are considered, the researcher may wish to weigh the benefits and limitations of using a topic guide or a questioning route. The researcher should then think about the process to use in developing the questions.

1

Guiding Principles of Asking Questions

As you think about questions, keep several guiding principles in mind. These are the foundation of all that follows.

Conversational-Conversational-Conversational

The first principle is to ask questions in a conversational manner. Because the focus group is a social experience, conversational questions are essential to create and maintain an informal environment. But what makes one question conversational and another awkward often depends on the situation.

The wording of the questions should be direct, forthright, comfortable, and simple. Are the questions easy to ask, or do you stumble over words? It is critical that the language is appropriate for the intended audience. Furthermore, the meaning of the question must be clearly conveyed orally. Some questions are

Language Must be Natural and Conversational for the Intended Audience

great when written but are confusing or stilted when asked orally. In addition, unneeded phrases at the beginning of a question can give confusing cues to the listener and distract from the intended purpose. The phrases or words intended to build the case for the question can also confuse the focus group participant or take the discussion off on a tangent. This occurs when the moderator offers lengthy background information on a question or uses a long segue from one topic to another.

Be Clear

Effective questions are clear, brief, and reasonable. Clear questions are usually short, one-dimensional, and jargon-free. Lengthy questions can be redundant or confusing to respondents. The risk of longer questions is that participants have a hard time distinguishing the core intent of the question. In general, you reduce clarity as the length of the question increases.

Another aspect of clarity is unidimensionality. The question should be limited to a single dimension. Moderators may inadvertently include words that they think are synonyms but that participants see as entirely different concepts. While the moderator means well, the participants get confused. For example, a question such as "In what ways was the program useful and practical?" may mean different things to different people. For some, "useful" and "practical" may be very different concepts.

At other times, moderators may add a second sentence or phrase that supposedly amplifies the question but in fact confuses the respondents by introducing another dimension, for example: "What is most important to you, that is, which topic should be acted upon first?" In this case, the moderator assumes that what is important should be acted upon first, but this may not be the view of participants.

A third aspect of clarity is wording. The words must be understandable to the participants. Acronyms, jargon, and technical language are deadly. Professionals are sometimes held captive by their language and inadvertently use technical terms or jargon confusing to lay audiences. Consequently, the questions should be reviewed by people similar to your target audience to make sure the language is clear.

I vividly remember a focus group question that bombed the first time it was used. It was an introductory question designed to get people talking. Instead, it got them confused. To the adult educators who developed the question, it seemed clear, but the participants felt differently. When the question was asked, "What was the most significant learning experience you've had in the past year?" the first person responded, "I have no idea what you are talking about!" The second person asked, "What is a significant learning experience?" The rest of the group was convinced that the moderator was an alien from another planet. The adult educators had loved the question, because this was the type of topic that they regularly think about, but to non-educators, it made no sense. Later we revised the question to read, "Tell us about something you learned last year that you found to be particularly enjoyable." The revised question worked well, and participants eagerly offered their answers.

—Richard Krueger

EXAMPLE

A Question That Didn't Work

Seek Help

Help is needed in developing quality focus group questions. No matter how talented a researcher may be, one individual developing questions alone will always be at a disadvantage. To ensure quality focus group questions, the researcher needs to obtain feedback from others. Often, the researcher and the intended audience have major differences in language. Therefore, input from people like the participants and advice from other researchers should be actively sought and considered.

Allow Sufficient Time

Quality questions are not produced quickly. The amount of time needed is often underestimated by the researcher and undervalued by the project sponsor. When the research sponsor reviews the proposed questioning route, the questions can seem so sensible and straightforward that a person might assume that questions are easy to develop. In some studies, the questioning route may have gone through half a dozen revisions before being seen by the research sponsors and then another six revisions before being used in the first focus group. Revisions take time, and the researcher must allow sufficient time for quality questions to emerge.

What Works Is Right

KEY POINT

There Is No One Right Way to Develop Questions. If It Works, It Is Right

A final guiding principle relates to finding out what is "right." Sometimes we get questions concerning the "right" way to develop questions for focus groups.

Our experience has been that this is an impossible question to answer, because experts may not know what is "right." Essentially, what is right is what works. Do the questions produce helpful results? If so, then they are right.

EXAMPLE

An Unexpectedly Valuable Question

Several years ago, we were conducting focus groups with farmers around the state. Technical colleges wanted to find out why farmers weren't attending their educational courses. I still remember reacting to a question that was suggested by a colleague. The suggested question was, "What would it take to get you to attend a training session at the area technical college?" Our initial reaction to the question was negative. It seemed too speculative and hypothetical, and we had never asked this question before. Although we had doubts, we agreed to try the question in the first focus group and see what happened. The day after the focus group, the moderator and assistant were really excited because the question turned out to be one of the most beneficial ones in the discussion. Farmers understood what was asked, they could indicate what was needed, and the results were of great benefit. We later used the same question in a number of studies with similar positive results.

With focus groups there is considerable interaction between moderator skills and effective questioning procedures. Some moderators can ask difficult questions while others asking these same questions find the participants cold and withdrawn. The moderator establishes a climate for communication, and participants develop a rapport based on trust and confidence. Without this trust the questions just aren't as effective. As a result, we find that what works for one moderator might not work for another. Find your own way, and if it works, continue using it. If it doesn't, make changes.

Let's be even more extreme. You may find some things in this book that run counter to your experiences. Perhaps we suggest a strategy that just hasn't been successful for you, or perhaps we discourage a technique that you've found productive. Again, the answer lies in what works for you. These principles have worked for us, and we hope they will work for you.

Naomi Henderson, a leading focus group researcher in marketing research, has offered 10 classic questions that have worked for her.

1. If you were in charge, what kind of changes would you make?
2. What would it take for this (product) to get a gold star? If this product received an award, what would it be for?
3. If you were the moderator, what would be the next question you would ask the group?
4. What would you tell a best friend or family member about this product?
5. Assume this product could talk, what would it say about itself?
6. If you could change one thing about this product, what would you change, and what's the main reason that one thing needs changing?
7. What would it take for this to get an A?
8. Can you tell me five positive things about this product, no matter how small that positive thing is?
9. If you were responsible for selling 1000 units of this product, what key point would you stress in the ad campaign?
10. What do you need to know about this product in order to accept or reject it?

—Henderson (1994)

**Ten Classic
Questions to
Ask in a
Focus Group**

2

The Topic Guide
Versus the
Questioning Route

Early in our experience with focus groups, we began by writing out the questions word for word. It just seemed like the right thing to do, and it never occurred to us that we might use an outline with key words. We also found that many moderators had the very opposite experience, beginning with an outline and never thinking about the benefits or potential of complete sentences.

Two different questioning strategies are currently in use, and each approach has built-in assumptions, advantages, and disadvantages. Think about which strategy you want to adopt.

The topic guide is a list of topics or issues to be pursued in the focus group. This list consists of words or phrases that remind the moderator of the topic of interest. By contrast, the questioning route is a sequence of questions in complete, conversational sentences.

EXAMPLE

**Topic Guide on
Quality Service**

1. Impression of "customer service"
2. Describe exceptionally good service
3. Describe poor service
4. Differences between public and private
5. Local office service compared with other public customer service
6. Write down three ingredients of customer service
7. Ingredient of fantastic service
8. Ingredient of awful service
9. Most important thing to keep doing
10. Missed anything

EXAMPLE

**Questioning
Route on
Quality Service**

1. In the last few years, we've often heard the words customer service. When you hear this term, what comes to mind?
2. Think about the last time you experienced exceptionally good service, regardless of where you had that experience. What happened that makes you describe your experience as exceptionally good service?
3. Think about a recent experience when you've received poor service. What happened that makes you describe your experience as poor?
4. Let's think about customer service in the public sector. How is it different from or similar to that of the private sector?
5. Let's talk specifically about the local offices of (name of local agency). How does the customer service there compare with other public sector or government agencies or organizations?
6. Take a piece of paper and write down three things that are important ingredients of customer service at the (name of local agency). Then, list three things that public organizations that provide excellent in customer service do. [WHEN FINISHED] OK, let's list these on the flip chart.
7. When you do business with (name of local agency), what is the single most important thing that could happen that would make you say that the service is fantastic?
8. On the other hand, what single thing could happen that might make you say that the service is just simply awful?
9. Think about all that we have talked about today. What do you think is most important for (name of local agency) to keep doing?
10. Have we missed anything?

The topic guide tends to be used by professional moderators in marketing research studies, whereas the questioning route is often preferred in the public, nonprofit, and academic environments. Let's consider the advantages and disadvantages of each approach.

Advantages of the Topic Guide

- Speed. Often topic guides can be developed more quickly than questioning routes.
- More conversational. Questions have a conversational tone because they are phrased in language comfortable and familiar to the moderator.
- Spontaneity. The topic guide may seem more spontaneous because it allows the moderator to reweave previous comments into future questions. This, however, requires skill.

Disadvantages of the Topic Guide

- More difficult analysis. Questions may be asked differently in different groups, and comparative analysis becomes difficult if not impossible. Sometimes slight changes in wording result in major changes in meaning.
- Limited feedback when pilot testing. The topic guide can be excessively cryptic with every reader making assumptions, sometime quite differently from each other, about what the words mean and how the words are put into complete sentences.
- Inconsistency between moderators. Different moderators will ask questions in different ways, sometimes with dramatically different meanings.

The topic guide approach requires the moderator to be skillful in spontaneously phrasing the topic into a coherent, single-dimension question presented as a complete sentence. This demands consistency and discipline by the moderator. As a result, we encourage beginning moderators to avoid the topic guide until mastery is achieved. The topic guide is more often used by people who do moderating for a living, and these experts have developed a sense of what will and won't work.

At its worst, the topic guide approach can be sloppy research and a disservice to both sponsors and the field of social science research. There is a greater tendency for individual differences to occur with the topic guide, and results can be unduly influenced by moderator behavior. However, some studies lend themselves to a topic guide approach, particularly when the concept is simple and straightforward, and the moderator is experienced.

We Encourage Beginning Moderators to Avoid the Topic Guide

Advantages of the Questioning Route

- Increased sponsor confidence. The questioning route tends to enhance sponsor confidence because the questions address the topics precisely as intended.
- Quality analysis. The questioning route produces more efficient analysis because it minimizes subtle differences in questions that could alter the intent.
- Enhanced consistency. The questioning route is preferred when different moderators are working on the same project.

Disadvantages of the Questioning Route

- Awkwardness. Unless the moderator is comfortable with the questions, the questions can seem stilted, insincere, and lacking in spontaneity.
- Slower to develop. Complete questions take longer to prepare to achieve the exact content desired by the sponsor.
- Potential false impression. A list of complete questions may give the sponsor the impression that you will ask the question "exactly" as written, which is often not the case.

3

How and Where to Begin

Sequence for Developing Questions

Overview

Clarify the Problem
Begin to Identify Questions
Prepare First Draft of Questions
Share and Revise, Revise, Revise

In the past, we relied on experts who worked alone to come up with the right questions and strategies for getting the answers. We've since learned that the key to good focus group research is to work with others to create the right questions. We'd like to suggest a process that we've found helpful, but don't feel that this is the only way to develop questions.

This approach taps into the expertise of different types of people through different roles: team leader, research team members, and brainstorming team members. The team leader is the researcher with lead responsibility for the project. Research team members are those assisting with planning and conducting the focus group study. The brainstorming team can include members of the research team but should also tap into the experiences and insights of those not familiar with research or the topic under investigation.

Clarify the Problem

The team leader takes responsibility and provides leadership for getting in touch with the problem. He or she asks questions, listens attentively, and thinks about how the problem is seen by others. Listen carefully as the research sponsor describes the problem. Ask for an explanation of how the problem developed and how the problem is seen by various groups or individuals. Don't assume that what you hear from the sponsor is the only way to describe the situation, but rather that it has meaning for those talking with you.

What has worked well for us is to hold a discussion (1 or 2 hours in length) with the research sponsors and the research team. Usually we limit the group to four to six people because we want not only efficiency but also multiple views and different approaches. Often these first discussions are freewheeling. We spend about half the time learning more about the problem, identifying the target audience, or even considering alternative research strategies. Then we use a brainstorming process to identify potential questioning strategies. Sometimes, we suggest a research strategy other than focus groups if another method seems more appropriate. A common dilemma is that the research sponsor wants to use focus groups to find solution strategies when attention should be placed on better understanding the problem from various perspectives. At the end of this discussion, the researchers are better able to develop a proposal that will address the problem described by the sponsor.

Begin to Identify Questions

Once the problem is understood and everyone has agreed that focus groups are appropriate, the next step is to gather ideas about questions that will shed light on the problem. Sometimes, the questioning strategy will be straightforward, and we'll know immediately where to begin. Other times, it's hard to decide where to begin because no particular way seems appropriate. When this occurs, we often use brainstorming.

Brainstorming works well with a group of four to six people. The leader of the group provides an overview of the problem and a description of the intended participants in the focus group, inviting suggestions for questions. Often, the discussion goes beyond identifying questions and circles back to issues about what type of participants should be included in the focus groups and about further clarification of the problem. The leader may push the group to avoid becoming locked into one way of thinking and to identify different ways to approach the problem. Someone is asked to write down the ideas shared. Often the team leader or the person who takes primary leadership for developing the questions assumes this role.

The goal of these brainstorming sessions is to generate a variety of ideas from which you will develop the final questions. Don't worry about the exact wording or phrasing or how the questions flow. Remember, at this point your goal is to get ideas, not the exact questions. Sometimes, the team members arrive at consensus on the questioning strategy, and other times they do not. The process is often fun, loud, and chaotic.

When putting together this brainstorming team, consider the benefits of diversity and the limits of similar experiences. The process often works best when the participants vary in background, knowledge of the topic, and experiences. Include generalists and specialists. Consider including people who resemble the potential participants in terms of age, ethnicity, experiences, or other factors.

Prepare First Draft of Questions

Prepare the first draft of questions as soon as possible after the brainstorming discussion. Often the team leader develops the draft. This is the time when attention is placed on the phrasing and sequencing of the questions. Until now, we have been trying to identify concepts, not obtain exact wording of the questions.

With a 2-hour limit, the researchers are restricted to about a dozen questions (plus or minus four). This rule of thumb obviously depends on the nature of the questions, as some questions can be answered literally in seconds, with no additional discussion needed. One strategy is to think of your questions as either 5-minute questions, 10-minute questions, or 15-minute questions. The 5-minute questions occur at the beginning of the focus group to introduce the topic as participants get ready to delve into the core areas, or as short transition questions midway through the discussion. The 10-minute questions are the areas of central concern that drive the study. The 15-minute questions represent a sizable time investment and must be very important. In a 2-hour focus group, you should plan for 90 minutes of questions, since the session may not start exactly on time and some time will be needed at the end for the summary and final participant comments. For example, the researcher might plan for the following:

- four to six 5-minute questions
- four to six 10-minute questions
- zero to two 15-minute questions

Share and Revise, Revise, Revise

Share the draft with others for review and feedback. Usually we don't get people physically together to review these drafts. We fax, e-mail, or mail out the questions and ask individuals to review them. Give consideration to who provides feedback and when the feedback is provided. Consider this sequence:

1. Brainstorming team
2. Research team
3. Sponsor of the study
4. Potential participants

In some studies, the team leader may prefer to share the questions with the brainstorming team, research team, and sponsor simultaneously. Indeed, in some studies these may all be the same people. In larger studies, the team leader may want to share the questions and get feedback from one team before sharing it with another. The most critical feedback will be from the sponsor. You will want to have the best possible set of questions to share with those funding the study; therefore, feedback from the brainstorming and research teams should occur prior to solicitation of the sponsor's reactions. After obtaining feedback from the sponsor, the research team might review the draft again and field test the questions with potential participants.

Pilot Testing Is Described in Chapter 10

How to Test Your Questions

Test questions to see if they are conversational. First, say them aloud. Are they easy to ask, or do you stumble over words? Do you feel comfortable asking the questions? Next, have a conversation about the study with some people like the focus group participants. Invite these people to tea, coffee, or a meal. Ask them how they would respond to the questions. Ask how they themselves would ask the questions if they believe your questions sound awkward. Besides testing questions, you can also get reactions to your recruitment plan, incentives, and logistics at this point.

Keep Track of Your Revisions

When seeking feedback on questions, place the date at the bottom or top of each page to identify the revision. Don't be surprised if you have six to ten revisions before you have closure on the questions. The dates help the research team and sponsor keep revisions separate.

Feedback is a hallmark of quality, and the team leader should nurture and encourage divergent ideas and approaches. At some point, however, the team leader will need to make decisions on questions. Normally, this decision is prompted by limited time and the need to get the study under way. If there are strongly held alternate views, the team leader should keep them on file as a contingency approach, if needed, after the first focus groups.

The end result will be a dozen or so questions that capture the intent of the study. Here's an example of a questioning route.

---

1. What are you hearing people say about the extension work in your community?
2. What outcomes or results from extension have you observed or heard about?
3. Think back to an experience you've had with extension that was outstanding. Describe it. (Encourage storytelling.)
4. What has been your greatest disappointment with extension?
5. Who doesn't participate in extension programs?
6. Let's talk about needs of people in the community and efforts of extension to meet those needs. What needs are addressed most effectively by extension? What needs are being overlooked that extension should address?
7. What are people saying about extension's cooperative efforts with other organizations?
8. In recent years there has been increasing concern about accountability for all public programs. Taxpayers are concerned about what they are getting from their investment. What should extension do about accountability?
9. How would you measure extension's success?
10. Extension wants people more involved in designing, planning, conducting, and evaluating extension programs. Programs are better when local residents are involved as active partners. What will encourage active participation?
11. Think about all that we have talked about today. What do you think is most important for extension to keep doing?
12. Have we missed anything?

EXAGEMPLE

Focus Group Questions for a Customer Study for a State Cooperative Extension Service

Part II

The Art and Mechanics
of Asking Good Questions

In this section, we outline categories of questions, share strategies for phrasing and sequencing questions, and give tips for
getting additional information through probing and follow-up
questions. We also challenge you to consider the limitations of
your questions, from time constraints to cultural considerations.
In this section, we suggest ways to pilot test your questions. There
is a mechanical aspect to asking good questions, but there is also
an artistic aspect. The mechanical aspect enables the researcher
to identify good questions, but art is needed to present those questions effectively. Can the moderator skillfully reweave previous
comments into subsequent questions to maintain the smooth flow
of the conversation? Without the art, the questions are short,
blunt, and choppy.

4

Categories of
Questions

Overview

Opening Question
Introductory Questions
Transition Questions
Key Questions
Ending Questions
Putting the Parts Together

Different types of questions are used at different times during the focus group. Each type of question has a distinct purpose. Typically, a focus group will contain each type of question. A key feature of focus group research is that not all questions are equal. Some questions are trivial and exist only as a prelude to a more important question. Other questions are of the utmost importance. The level of importance influences the amount of time spent on the question as well as the intensity of the analysis. Not all questions are analyzed in the same way. Some questions, such as the opening question, may not be analyzed at all. The moderator may move through some questions rapidly, whereas other questions will need a leisurely discussion.

Essentially there are five categories of questions, each with a distinctive function in the flow of a focus group interview. We call these question categories: opening, introductory, transition, key, and ending. For the sake of thoroughness, these questions are presented as a questioning route, not as a topic guide.

KEY POINT

**Some Questions
Are More
Important
Than Others**

Categories of Questions	
Question Type	Purpose
Opening	Participants get acquainted and feel connected
Introductory	Begins discussion of topic
Transition	Moves smoothly and seamlessly into key questions
Key	Obtains insight on areas of central concern in the study
Ending	Helps researchers determine where to place emphasis and brings closure to the discussion

Remember the Big Idea of the Categories

We offer these five categories of questions merely as suggestions—not as ironclad rules. These categories are intended to be used as general guidelines, not absolute strategy. The major contribution of the categories is helping the researcher sequence and bring focus to the questions. Novice moderators tend to move too quickly into key questions, and the premature discussion of these can miss critical concepts. Often, the questions can be improved by using these principles. If you are a beginning moderator, give careful thought to these categories. If you are an experienced moderator, you might use these categories as diagnostic aids when your questioning strategy isn't working as well as you'd like.

Insights Into Successful Community Heart Health Programs

Opening   1. Tell us your name and where you live.

Introduction   2. Describe a healthy person.

Transition   3. When you think of Heart Health, what comes to mind?

Transition   4. Think back to the past several years. Have you made any changes in your diet, exercise, or personal habits? Tell us about them.

Key   5. What prompted these changes?
FOLLOW-UP:
Friends, family, and neighbors
Written information
Media messages
Medical advice
Physical health
Personal desire to change

Key   6. Which of those mentioned was most influential?

Key   7. Tell us about the things you tried to do but discontinued; the changes you tried to make but were not successful.

Ending   8. We are trying to help people make healthy changes. What advice do you have for us?

Let's consider each of these types of focus group questions in more detail.

Opening Question

Everyone answers the opening question at the beginning of the focus group. It is designed to be answered quickly (usually in about 30 seconds) and to make people feel comfortable by identifying characteristics that participants have in common. Usually it is preferable for these questions to be based on facts as opposed to attitudes or opinions of participants. Questions of attitude or opinion take time to answer, require examples or stories, and beg for discussion. The opening question is not a discussion question but strictly a process to encourage everyone to talk early in the group. Attitude and opinion questions are better placed later in the focus group discussion.

The opening question is usually not intended to obtain useful information for the study. Indeed, some factual information that might seem easy and fast to obtain can actually work against you—such as educational level, size of business, professional qualifications, etc. Questions intended to elicit such information emphasize how people are different from one another, as opposed to how they are alike. The only condition when these might be used is when the moderator knows ahead of time with great confidence that all respondents will give similar answers. More often, this type of demographic information is requested in a short written "registration form" or "background survey" when participants arrive at the focus group site if it is really needed.

Opening questions are typically not analyzed. The intent of the question is to establish a sense of community in the group in terms of how participants feel after they've heard responses from others. One of the best opening questions that I've heard was asked of a group of dentists. It was: "Tell us who you are, where you practice dentistry, and what you most enjoy doing when you're not practicing dentistry." The question established that all of the participants had dentistry in common and that they were practitioners and human beings with interests, hobbies, and families.

Opening Questions

- *"Tell us your name, where you practice dentistry, and what you most enjoy doing when you're not practicing dentistry."*
- *"Tell us who you are, where you live, and your favorite memory of last summer."*
- *"Tell us your name and tell us about a gift that was memorable to you. This gift could have been one that you've either given or received. It could have been recent or long ago."*
- *"Tell us your name and one thing you'd like us to know about your child—one thing that your child does that makes you smile."*

Introductory Questions

Introductory questions introduce the general topic of discussion and/or provide participants with an opportunity to reflect on experiences and their connection with the overall topic. The questions foster conversation and interaction among the participants but are not critical to analysis.

While the opening question gets participants to talk, it is the introductory question that begins the focus on the topic. Typically, this is an open-ended question that allows participants to tell about how they see or understand the phenomenon under investigation. The question could ask for a definition, an explanation, or an overview of how people have experienced a product or service. Sometimes, the introductory question asks participants to remember when they first experienced or encountered the organization or topic under investigation. This introductory question begins to give the moderator clues about the participants' reality. It is sometimes helpful to reweave these clues into the discussion later in the focus group. Occasionally, participants will offer answers to introductory questions that are completely unanticipated. These unique insights may lead to additional probing or follow-up questions.

Introductory Questions

- *"When you hear the words customer service, what comes to mind?"*
- *"What's your first impression of the Minnesota Extension Service?"*
- *"What persuaded you to join the agency?"*

Transition Questions

Transition questions move the conversation toward the key questions that drive the study. The transition questions help participants envision the topic in a broader scope. They serve as the logical link between the introductory questions and the key questions. During these questions the participants are becoming aware of how others view the topic. These questions set the stage for productive key questions.

Often, transition questions ask participants to go into more depth than introductory questions about their experiences and use of a product. While the introductory question brings the topic to the surface, the transition questions make the connection between the participant and the topic of investigation.

- *"How have you been involved with community education?"*
- *"Tell us about courses you've had to improve your skills."*
- *"What are the benefits of working in this agency?"*

EXAMPLE

Transition Questions

Key Questions

Key questions drive the study. Typically, there are two to five questions in this category. These are usually the first questions to be developed by the research team and the ones that require the greatest attention in the analysis.

It's crucial for the moderator to know which questions are key questions. The moderator needs to allow sufficient time for a full discussion of these questions. Although only a few minutes might be allocated for each of the earlier questions, the key questions may need as much as 10 or 15 minutes each. Furthermore, the moderator will likely need to use pauses and probes more frequently with key questions. Key questions usually begin about one third to one half of the way into the focus group.

GO TO

For More Information on the Usefulness of Pauses, See Chapter 4 of *Moderating Focus Groups*

EXAMPLE

Key Questions

- *"Tell me about the things you tried to do but discontinued; the changes you tried to make but were not successful."*
- *"What role did others have in your success?"*
- *"What helped you continue the change?"*
- *"What would get you to participate in this program?"*
- *"Suppose you were trying to encourage a friend to participate in this program. What would you say?"*

Ending Questions

These questions bring closure to the discussion, enable participants to reflect on previous comments, and are critical to analysis. These questions can be of three types: the all-things-considered question, the summary question, and the final question.

All-Things-Considered Questions

At the end of the focus group, you may use a question that allows participants to state their final position on critical areas of concern. We call this the "all-things-considered" question. It allows each participant to reflect on all comments shared in the discussion and then to identify which aspects are most important, most in need of action, etc. Also, individuals may have shared inconsistent points of view, and this question allows them to clarify their position at the conclusion of the discussion. Often, this question is answered by each person in the group.

EXAMPLE

All-Things-Considered Questions

- *"Suppose you had one minute to talk to the governor on the topic of merit pay. What would you say?"*
- *"Of all the needs we discussed, which one is most important to you?"*
- *"Jot down on a piece of paper one phrase or one sentence that best describes your position on this topic."*

This type of question is helpful in analysis because it is used to interpret conflicting comments and assign weight to what was said. Sometimes, trivial concerns are talked about with frequency, and it's a serious mistake for the analyst to assume that frequency reflects importance. If the analyst wants to know what participants consider important, then that question must be explicitly asked of participants, ideally as an ending question.

Summary Question

The summary question is asked after the moderator or assistant moderator has given a short oral summary (2 or 3 minutes) of the key questions and the big ideas that emerged from the discussion. After the summary, the participants are asked about the adequacy of the summary. This question also plays a critical role in analysis.

Chapter 4 of *Moderating Focus Groups* has more information on the use of pauses

- *"Is this an adequate summary?"*
- *"Did I correctly describe what was said?"*
- *"How well does that capture what was said here?"*

EXAMPLE

Summary Questions

1. Before the focus group, be sure you know the key questions and the approximate time the moderator plans to spend on each key question.
2. Be clear in your mind about the purpose of the focus group. The summary should tie closely to this purpose.
3. Take notes with two things in mind: first, notes that will help you provide a brief oral summary and, second, notes for your detailed analysis after the focus group.
4. Begin your oral summary with the most important findings, regardless of when they were discussed in the focus group. Don't worry about the question sequence when you construct your summary.
5. Begin your summary with findings—what was actually said. Attempt to capture common themes but also acknowledge differing points of view. This descriptive summary repeats what was said but is very brief. After you've given the summary of what was said, consider offering an interpretation. The interpretive summary attaches additional meaning and goes beyond the actual words.
6. Listen for what was not said but might have been expected. If these areas are important, then in the summary you might say, "Some things were not mentioned like . . . and I am assuming they are not important." Look at the participants while you're saying this and watch for reactions.
7. Cite key phrases used in the discussion. This demonstrates connectedness and careful listening.
8. Keep the summary to 3 minutes or less. If you ramble on, people will tune out.
9. When finished, look at the participants and ask, "Is this summary complete?" or "Does this sound OK to you?"

TIP

How to Give an Oral Summary at the End of the Focus Group

Final Question

The final question in a focus group is an "insurance question." Its unique purpose is to ensure that critical aspects have not been overlooked. The question begins with a short overview of the purpose of the study. This overview may be slightly longer and more descriptive than what was said in the advance letter or oral introduction to the focus group. Following this overview, the moderator asks the final question: Has anything been missed?

EXAMPLE

Final Questions

- *"Have we missed anything?"*
- *"Is there anything that we should have talked about but didn't?"*

For this question to work effectively, there must be sufficient time remaining at the conclusion of the focus group. It is best to have about 10 minutes remaining before the promised adjournment time. This question is particularly important at the beginning of a series of focus groups to ensure that the questioning route is logical and complete. This final question can also be used to get feedback on your moderating skills. If something isn't working, the participants are often willing to tell you if you ask with a smile and explain that you want to improve. We sometimes explain, "This is the first in a series of groups that we are doing. Do you have any advice on how we can improve?"

Putting the Parts Together

Now let's put these components together into a set of questions. Here are several examples of focus group questions. The first example is from a not-for-profit organization that wanted to design an educational program to help local residents lower their cholesterol. Before they designed the program, they wanted to find out more about what information people wanted, how they liked to get information, and how to keep people motivated in continuing with cholesterol reduction.

Opening	1. Tell us your name and where you live.
Introduction	2. What to you is good health?
Transition	3. What to you is a healthy lifestyle?
Key	4. Think back to the last time you wanted to make a change relating to health. It may have been a change in what you eat, your weight, smoking, or exercise habits. What kind of barriers or roadblocks did you run into?
Key	5. What helped you or would have helped you the most in making the change?
Transition	6. Suppose you have been told by your doctor that your cholesterol level is too high. What would you want to know, or what kind of information would you like to get?
Key	7. Some of you mentioned foods and diet. Let's talk about that. What kind of information would you want to get about foods and your diet to help you lower your cholesterol?
Key	8. There are a lot of different ways you could get the types of information you have just been talking about. How would you like to get that information?
Key	9. Of all those ways of getting information, which do you feel is most important?
Key	10. Suppose that a workshop on cholesterol was held. What would get you to attend?
Key	11. We realize that it's hard to stay motivated to learn about things like cholesterol, but what would entice you to come back for more? What would keep you interested?
Ending	12. We are going to be putting together programs for residents on how to lower their cholesterol. As we begin this project, what advice do you have for us?

EXAMPLE

Questions on Cholesterol Changes

The second example was used to determine how to develop a community wellness campaign. The results helped experts design workable strategies that were based on past successes.

EXAMPLE

Success Factors in Community Wellness

Opening	1.	Tell us your first name and your favorite food.
Introduction	2.	You have been selected because you've made a positive change in your health. Each of you has changed one or more things in your lifestyle. Briefly tell us what you did.
Transition	3.	Where did you get the idea for the change?
Key	4.	After you got the idea, did you seek more information?
Key	5.	What role did others have in your success?
Key	6.	What slowed you up?
Key	7.	What helped you continue the change?
Ending	8.	What advice would you give to others considering the change?
Ending	9.	We would like to help others become successful in making healthy changes. What advice do you have for us?

The next example was used to test draft materials in a violence prevention campaign and to obtain suggestions that would make the program successful.

EXAMPLE

Pilot Test Materials and Strategies

Opening	1.	Tell us who you are and where you live.
Introduction	2.	What kinds of violence are in the lives of young people?
Transition	3.	Take a few moments and look over the materials for parents on preventing violence. The first part is a draft copy of a parent guide for preventing violence. The second part includes suggestions for community-based activities.
		PAUSE FOR PARENTS TO REVIEW MATERIALS
Key	4.	What was your first impression of these materials?
Key	5.	What one thing do you like the best about these materials?
Key	6.	What one thing do you like the least?
Key	7.	Were there any parts of this material that seemed inappropriate?
Key	8.	Were there any parts of this material that other parents might be concerned about?
Key	9.	What would get you to participate in this effort?
Key	10.	Suppose that you were trying to encourage a friend to participate in this program. What would you say?
Ending	11.	If you could change one thing about the program, what would it be?
Ending	12.	Do you have any other advice for us as we introduce these new materials or this campaign?

5

Phrasing the Questions

Overview

Use Open-Ended Questions
Ask Participants to Think Back
Avoid Asking Why
Keep Questions Simple
Be Cautious About Giving Examples

After brainstorming the topics or questions, the researcher phrases questions in language appropriate for participants. Let's consider the strategies for phrasing questions.

Use Open-Ended Questions

Perhaps the most distinctive feature of the focus group interview is the open-ended questions. Indeed, it is difficult to imagine a focus group without open-ended questions. Open-ended questions allow the respondents to determine the direction of the response. The answer is not implied, and the type or manner of response is not suggested. Individuals are encouraged to respond based on their specific situation. The major advantage of the open-ended question is that it reveals what is on the interviewee's mind, as opposed to what the interviewer suspects is on the

KEY POINT

Open-Ended Questions Are Essential for Focus Group Interviews

interviewee's mind. Closed-ended questions aren't totally off-limits, however. Toward the end of the group interview, it may be productive to narrow the types of responses and bring greater focus to the answers by shifting to closed-ended questions,

Some questions are deceptive and appear to be open-ended but are really closed-ended questions in disguise. Questions that include words like *satisfied, to what extent,* or *how much* imply answers that fall within a specified range such as *very satisfied, to some extent,* or *a great deal.* These questions are usually used toward the latter part of the interview as the moderator narrows the range of inquiry. Bounding the questions may be helpful to a moderator trying to regain control of a rambling discussion or in situations where the topic requires more specific insights.

EXAMPLE

Open-Ended Questions

- *"What did you think of the program?"*
- *"How did you feel about the conference?"*
- *"Where do you get new information?"*
- *"What do you like best about the proposed program?"*

It is possible to add structure by delimiting or bounding the question while still allowing respondents to select their own way of answering, such as:

- *"What did you think of the part of the program that described new farming techniques?"*
- *"How did you feel about Dr. Jones' presentation at the conference?"*
- *"Where do you get new information on parenting skills?"*
- *"What do you like best about how the new program is promoted?"*
- *"Which of these three designs do you like best?"*

Ask Participants to Think Back

The "think back" question asks participants to reflect on their personal experiences and then respond to a specific question. "Think back to when you began working at the public health service. What attracted you to the position?" Or, "Think back to the last time you registered for a course at the university. How were you treated?" The "think back" phrase helps establish a context for the response. These words let participants know that you want them to be specific and grounded in their experiences, as opposed to repeating "hearsay" from others or just stating community beliefs and values.

There's a tendency for participants to respond to the more immediate interviewing experience—the here and now—unless you ask them to shift themselves to another place in time. This focus on the past increases the reliability of the responses because it asks about specific experiences as opposed to current intentions or future possibilities. The question asks what the person has done as opposed to what might be done in the future. The shift is from what might be, or ought to be, to what has actually been. This time shift cues the respondent to speak from experience, as opposed to wishes and intentions.

Avoid Asking Why

"Why" questions imply a rational answer, one developed by thought and reflection. Unfortunately, these questions present problems, because in real life, people make decisions based on impulse, habit, tradition, or other nonrational processes. When asked "why," respondents provide answers that seem rational or appropriate to the situation. Unfortunately, the answers received may not be reliable. The answers may sound good, seem reasonable, and, on the surface, appear to be right. In fact, that's why these answers are often given, because they sound good and seem reasonable. The participant has "intellectualized" the answer, speaking from the brain and not from deeper forces that motivate behavior.

Moreover, the "why" question has sharpness or pointedness to it that reminds people of interrogations. This sharpness raises defensive barriers, and the respondent tends to take a position on the socially acceptable side of controversial issues.

If the researcher decides to use a "why" question, it should be specific. Paul Lazarfeld (1986) has called this the principle of specification. Lazarfeld's principle of specification is that such questions are answered in one of two ways. When asked why, the respondent may respond on (1) the basis of "influences" that prompted the action or (2) the basis of certain desirable "attributes."

Let's use Lazarfeld's model to examine responses to a seemingly simple question: "Why did you go to the zoo?"

Influence Answer: "Because my kids really wanted to go."
Attribute Answer: "Because I wanted to see the Beluga whale."

What seems like a straightforward and simple question can really be answered on several dimensions. The first answer describes an influence, while the second relates to a feature or attribute of the zoo. A preferable strategy is to break the "why" question down into different questions, for example:

Influence: "What prompted (influenced, caused, made) you to go to the zoo?" Or

Attribute: "What features of the zoo do you particularly like?"

A less direct approach is to ask people "what" or "how" they feel about the subject of discussion. Often, people can describe the feelings they had when they considered using a particular product or program. In addition, they can probably describe the anticipated consequences of using the product or program.

Keep Questions Simple

Beginning researchers tend to make focus group questions too complex. Simple questions and clarity of thought are essential. For example, don't ask, "What are the ingredients that are associated with healthy living?" Instead ask, "Describe a healthy lifestyle." Think of the shortest way to ask the question clearly. The best focus group questions are simply stated. When these questions are asked, the participants immediately know what is asked for, and within seconds, they are on their way to providing an answer. By contrast, the killer questions are those that have multiple interpretations. Participants hesitate to respond because the question is confusing. Then, while thinking, they become distracted by the comments of other participants and forget their train of thought.

Simple questions do not yield simple answers! It is often the simple question that gets the participant to bring shape and form to the discussion. It pulls out assumptions and lays bare the core principles. You can spot the simple questions because they typically have few words, no jargon or inside language, and no commas, semicolons, or hyphens. The simple question is not condescending or childish. It's a sophisticated question that get at the core of the topic.

Perhaps the most distinctive feature of simple questions is that they are memorable. Participants may often forget the question if it is too complex. The memorable question is one that continues to "ring" in their heads. Even if someone gets off topic, another participant remembers the question and brings the discussion back on track.

Be Cautious About Giving Examples

Examples are like mental ruts. Although they provide ideas for the type of response, they also limit the thinking of respondents. The danger to the researcher is that these examples give clues to the type of response that might be offered. Suppose you are doing a study of customer satisfaction; because the topic is broad, you decide to use the example of how complaints are handled. Well, handling complaints is only one facet of customer satisfaction, but because it evokes memories and vivid experiences, it can dominate the conversation and prevent other dimensions from emerging. If you do give examples, give them as probes after participants have already given their insights. See if these examples expand the conversation.

In a similar vein, the comments or ideas of some participants can trap and limit the thinking of other participants. Vivid examples, compelling stories, or emotional experiences can easily redirect the conversation and thinking of participants. If this begins to occur, the moderator should repeat the original question, thereby refocusing the discussion on the original intent.

6

Sequencing the Questions

Overview

Provide Background Information to Participants
General Questions Before Specific Questions
Positive Questions Before Negative Questions
Uncued Questions Before Cued Questions
Participant Categories Before Other Categories

Focus group questions are not just thrown together. With care and thoughtfulness, the researcher arranges a questioning sequence. This question sequence is a hallmark of focus group interviews and the reason that we use the word *focus* in the title. This focused sequence makes sense to participants, and it provides an opportunity for them to anchor their opinions and then build on those views. The first few questions in the focus group discussion allow participants to reflect and think of experiences with the study topic, for example, When and where did they have the experience? How did they feel about it? While participants reflect and talk about their experiences, they are also listening to others tell of their experiences. This listening process is a distinctive feature of focus group interviews. In other research procedures, participants are rarely aware of the views and experiences of others. In focus group interviews, the participants can listen to opinions and experiences of others. Moreover, they can com-

KEY POINT

The Sequence of Questions Is a Hallmark of Focus Group Interviewing

ment, disagree with, or build upon those comments. This focus group strategy is deliberate because it helps participants remember their own experiences and then compare and contrast their experiences with those of others. As a result, the first questions in the focus group become a foundation upon which later discussion is built.

Provide Background Information to Participants

The moderator must provide consistent background information to each participant about the purpose of the study in order to minimize tacit assumptions. In interview situations, respondents make assumptions about the nature of the questions and then answer accordingly. These tacit assumptions are vexing because the respondent may be providing an answer based on faulty assumptions. Paul Lazarfeld provides an illustration of tacit assumption from a detective story by G. K. Chesterton (1951).

> Have you ever noticed this—that people never answer what you say? They answer what you mean—or what they think you mean. Suppose one lady says to another in a country house, "Is anybody staying with you?" the lady doesn't answer "Yes; the butler, the three footmen, the parlourmaid, and so on," though the parlourmaid may be in the room, or the butler behind her chair. She says "There is nobody staying with us," meaning nobody of the sort you mean. But suppose a doctor inquiring into an epidemic asks, "Who is staying in the house?" then the lady will remember the butler, the parlourmaid, and the rest. All language is used like that; you never get a question answered literally, even when you get it answered truly. (p. 98)

All information given in preparation for the discussion helps develop the tacit knowledge of participants. The moderator should be careful so that all advance communication ensures uniformity, consistency, and sufficient generality regarding the purposes of the discussion.

Focus group participants usually want to know the purpose of the session. They may wonder why the session is being held, who the sponsor is, or how the information is going to be used. These topics can be discussed during the invitation phase or at the beginning of the focus group. This information provides clues to respondents about how or in what manner they might respond. It should also provide enough information so that participants feel comfortable sharing their thoughts. Expert moderators are careful to make the introduction smooth and snappy. There is no redundancy, and, as quickly as possible, the moderator engages participants in the discussion.

General Questions Before Specific Questions

The most common procedure in arranging questions is to go from general to specific—that is, beginning with general overview questions that funnel into more specific questions of critical interest. Avoid presenting participants with specific questions without first establishing the context created by more general questions. For example, suppose a series of focus group interviews will be held with young people. The purpose is to learn their perceptions of youth organizations and eventually to identify an effective means of advertising a particular organization. It would be premature to begin with questions on advertising the organization. Instead, the moderator might ask the participants to describe their favorite youth organization or to describe what they like about youth clubs. Later in the discussion, the moderator might narrow the topic to focus on a specific youth organization under investigation. Perhaps toward the end of the discussion, the moderator might solicit opinions on several different approaches that are being considered for advertising the youth group.

An actual illustration of the general-to-specific technique of focusing questions comes from Hawaii. To gain insights into how consumers use Kona coffee, the moderator began with questions about gourmet foods and then asked about gourmet beverages. When a participant suggested Kona coffee, the moderator then encouraged discussion of how and when this type of coffee was used.

The funnel analogy is useful because it presents the researcher with a sequential strategy for arranging questions. The funneling concept is used to move the discussion from broad to narrow, from general to specific, or from abstract to specific. The funneling begins with fairly broad discussion and is followed by a series of narrower, more focused questions. Steadily, the questions become more and more focused, and eventually there are several that exactly hit the target of the inquiry.

Positive Questions Before Negative Questions

A questioning strategy that works well asks participants to comment on both positive and negative experiences or observations. It is interesting that this strategy works better when the first request is for positive items as opposed to negative ones. Perhaps this reflects our mothers' exhortation that we shouldn't say something bad unless we've first said something good.

The benefit of using both positive and negative questions is that this strategy allows participants to comment on both sides of the issue—and in some situations this is particularly important. At times, focus group participants get in a rut and become excessively critical of the topic of investigation. This seems to occur when all participants have common and sometimes unpleasant bonding experiences. It's reasonable for employees of an organization, students in an educational setting, or military personnel to launch into criticism of those who have control and power. Moreover, in some settings, participants attempt to outdo each other with bizarre, extreme, or outlandish experiences. In situations where participants begin with negative features and tend to dwell on the undesirable factors, there is value in "turning the tables" and asking for opposite views: "So what are the benefits of working around here?" "What's positive about being a student?" and so forth.

Often, the transition from positive to negative aspects proceeds smoothly and comfortably, but care is needed so that it isn't premature. One rather predictable scenario is that, while positive attributes are being discussed, a participant might disagree with the positive statement and want to offer a contrary point of view. This can easily lead to discussion of negative attributes without further exploration of other positive ones. Here, the moderator will need to exercise mild control and encourage the group to stick to the positive attributes before shifting to the less desirable features.

Uncued Questions Before Cued Questions

The moderator often faces a dilemma in the questioning route. In some questions, the moderator is seeking new ideas, approaches, or examples from the participants. When examples are provided by the moderator, they can limit or restrict the thinking of participants. A better approach is to begin by asking the question without providing a cue—the uncued question. The uncued question is open-ended, but it is also so all-encompassing that participants may have a little difficulty in providing lengthy commentary. Typically, the responses will be based on participants' most recent or vivid experiences or impressions. The rule of thumb is to ask the uncued question first and then follow up with cues to prompt additional discussion. After the topics have been discussed in a general way, the moderator might then offer some cues and ask for comments. If the moderator does not offer cues and a certain topic is not mentioned, then it is impossible to determine if a point was left out due to an oversight or if it was just not important. Only by offering cues can the moderator determine the difference. The cues themselves require some thought. They are developed before the focus group and limited in number yet reasonably exhaustive. They should be general enough to allow for a variety of comments and specific enough to prompt ideas and thoughts. Note the example below.

In a community needs assessment, the participants were asked to identify what was needed by local residents. The moderator found that initial comments from individuals came from those who had given this topic previous thought or who had relevant recent or vivid experiences. These most recent or vivid experiences are like first impressions in that they tend to be unstable and change as the discussion ensues. After a while, the discussion lagged, and the moderator offered cues. The moderator held up a list of categories as cues to the participants, stating, "Here is a list of topics that might help us think of needs within the community. It includes: family, transportation, health, safety, recreation, youth, seniors. After looking at this list, are there any additional needs that come to mind?" The resulting discussion helped identify a valuable list of community needs.

EXAMPLE

Uncued and Cued Questions

When using uncued and cued questions, it may also be helpful to include an all-things-considered question, described earlier. In this question, the participants are asked to identify the one factor (need, concern, etc.) that they consider to be the most important (critical, necessary to address, etc.). Responses to this question greatly aid the analysis. An analysis error sometimes made in focus groups is to assume that what is most frequently mentioned is also most important. A far less risky approach is to include a specific question to allow the participants to comment on what they consider to be most important. This all-things-considered question is often invaluable in later analysis.

Participant Categories Before Other Categories

In some studies, the researcher wants focus group participants to rate, rank, or comment on approaches, items, strategies, etc., developed by those outside of the focus group. These could be lists developed by experts or past research. Usually, the preferable sequencing strategy is to begin by asking participants to identify their own categories before considering categories from other sources. It's too easy for participants to find themselves trapped in the approaches and assumptions of others.

Importance of Obtaining Participant Responses

Recently, a university conducted a study of water quality in a river basin. The intent was to find out the research needs of farmers and others living in the area. Researchers at the university had already listed preferred research topics, based on their expertise. The questioning strategy was to ask focus group participants to identify areas of research that would be important to them, before they looked at the list prepared by university researchers. Interestingly enough, the lists in this study were quite different. In fact, researchers had based their list on an assumed cause-effect relationship between certain agricultural practices and water quality, whereas farmers discounted the assumption that agricultural practices were the major influence on water quality in the river basin.

Several strategies can be used in developing a list of categories. One is to ask participants to make their own list. Participants can just suggest topics orally, or you could have each person take a moment and list several items on a piece of paper that is then shared with the entire group. A strategy that often works well is to ask participants to list two or three items on a piece of paper, go around the table, and have each person read his or her list, using a flip chart to record responses for all to see. It's important to have participants actually jot down their choices in writing before sharing these orally with others. There is a tendency in some groups for participants not to share their thoughts if they feel intimidated, if they feel their choices are of lesser value, or if their items seem redundant. The written list ensures that all entries are captured. Another variation to developing the list is to meld the participants' nominations with the researcher's list without calling attention to the source of each item. The researcher's list might be developed from a review of research, from expert opinions, or from earlier focus groups. Sometimes, the researcher's list tends to take on the "official and correct aura" if it is introduced separately. To counter this tendency, the moderator announces, "We are in the process of developing categories, and we want to be certain that we've included all of those that are important. Each participant will be asked to make a list, and these will help in developing the larger master list." The assistant moderator collects participants' lists along with the researcher's list, eliminates duplication, and quickly develops a flip chart for discussion.

Several strategies are possible to determine quickly which factors are most important (most helpful, most immediate, etc.). The moderator might ask each person to look over the list on the flip chart and pick one item that he or she considers to be the most important. Again, go around the table so that everyone can suggest his or her "most important" factor. Another process that works well but takes slightly longer is to ask each participant to rate the importance of every item, using a scale of four or five points. Participants write the name of each item on a piece of paper along with their rating of importance. These can be collected and tabulated silently by the assistant moderator, thereby preserving the confidentiality of each respondent, or orally by just asking all participants to announce their scores.

When participants have made their lists, these can be compared with those of experts. Usually, it is preferable to tell participants that the second list was prepared by "others" or "people who are concerned about this issue," rather than saying that it was prepared by experts. Then participants can look over both listings and pick out what they consider the best of both lists.

7

Probes, Follow-Ups, and Unplanned Questions

Overview
Probe Questions
Follow-Up Questions
Unplanned or Serendipitous Questions

Probe Questions

In many conversations and group discussions, people make cryptic or vague comments that could have multiple meanings. Sometimes, this is done intentionally, but other times, the speaker may be unaware of multiple interpretations. The probe is an effective technique to elicit additional information.

EXAMPLE

Probe Questions

- *"Would you explain further?"*
- *"Can you give me an example?"*
- *"Would you say more?"*
- *"Is there anything else?"*
- *"Please describe what you mean."*
- *"I don't understand."*

KEY POINT

Probe Sparingly and Always Consider Potential Usefulness of Information

Successful probing requires thought and discipline by the moderator. Not everything is worthy of a probe, and too much probing provides excessive detail on trivial matters. Probes should be used sparingly. Before probing, the moderator should think about whether this information has potential usefulness in the study. The moderator must also weigh the time needed for the probe against the time available for other questions. Excessive probing stifles the group conversation, as when it becomes a two-way conversation between the moderator and one participant. Therefore, the moderator must use judgment about the timing and duration of probes.

Probing early in the discussion can be beneficial, sending a signal of the amount of detail sought by the moderator. It's a wise strategy to probe early in the focus group on a topic central to the study. This emphasizes to the participants the importance of precision in responses. When a participant just says, "I agree," the moderator should respond with, "Tell us more," or "What experiences have you had that make you feel that way?" A few probes used in this way underscore the impression that more detailed answers are needed and wanted.

Follow-Up Questions

Follow-up questions are those linked to the preceding question by logic or reason. Typically, the first question sets a baseline or establishes a set of conditions that are examined in more detail in the second part—the follow-up question. These two-part questions are connected by logic.

Follow-up questions are similar to probes in that the researcher is seeking additional information, but they are different in the sense that the follow-up questions are intentional and written into the questioning route. By contrast, probes are typically spontaneous. The follow-up question often follows an "if-then" style, where the researcher first asks a question to define or understand a problem or situation. This is followed by a question of opinion, interpretation, behavior, and so forth.

Follow-Up Questions	
If	*Then*
Facts	Opinions Interpretations Behaviors
Problems	Cause Resolution
Situation	Antecedents Consequences
Stimulus	Response

BACKGROUND

Style of Follow-Up Questions

The first question anchors the concept, and the second builds on it. An area for researchers to consider is whether they want these questions answered individually or as a group. Often, the follow-up question is asked of the entire group, with all participants encouraged to answer the first part before the second part is asked. This allows participants to hear how others perceive a situation and fosters a variety of insights.

- *"What are the needs within our community?" THEN "Which of these is the most important?"*
- *"What is the major problem in the community?" THEN "What are the causes?"*
- *"What's the greatest challenge facing youth today?" THEN "What should we do about it?"*
- *"Is violence is a growing concern in our schools? THEN "What should be done about it?"*

EXAMPLE

Follow-Up Questions

Unplanned or Serendipitous Questions

Occasionally, in the flow of a focus group interview, the moderator or assistant moderator thinks of a question that might be useful to the study. The question may never have occurred to the research team before the discussion, but the idea is prompted by the comments of participants. These serendipitous questions can be beneficial to the research, but it is often preferable to withhold them until near the end of the discussion. These unplanned questions may take the discussion off on a quite different trail of unknown consequences and thereby disrupt the comparability across groups. Unanticipated questions inserted in the middle of the discussion can waste precious minutes in a potentially unproductive route. Therefore, it is best to save serendipitous questions for the end of the focus group.

8

Know the Limits

Overview

Time and Attention Constraints
Clarity Constraints
Cultural Constraints
Language Constraints

As you develop focus group questions, it's wise to be aware of limits: constraints of time, attention, and clarity, plus cultural and language factors.

Time and Attention Constraints

Focus groups are typically 60 to 120 minutes long. Some successful groups have been conducted in less time, particularly with student groups or on narrowly focused studies. At the other extreme, we occasionally hear of focus groups lasting more than 2 hours. The 2-hour time limit, however, is a physical and psychological limit for most people. (Among the few exceptions are mock jury focus groups, which can last 8 hours.) Don't go beyond the 2-hour maximum unless there is a special event or circumstance that makes it comfortable for participants, such as providing lunch or dinner.

Don't Go Over Two Hours With Your Focus Group

Earlier, we talked about questions requiring different lengths of time. Some questions can be answered in a matter of seconds while others will demand more discussion. Consider the categories of questions and their time requirements when finalizing the questions. Also, give thought to the size of the focus group and the level of participant expertise. Generally speaking, as your focus group becomes larger or when participants are expert or knowledgeable about the topic, you will need to keep the number of questions to a minimum.

BACKGROUND

Categories of Questions and Time Requirements

Category of Questions	Time Requirement
Facts	Very brief. Sometimes less than 60 seconds
Examples and Stories	Moderate. Can range from 5 to 10 minutes
Discussion, Compare and Contrast	Long. Range from 10 to 15 minutes
Activities, Involvement, Reflection, Sharing	Very long. Often more than 15 minutes

Clarity Constraints

Conceptual clarity is essential. The research team must have a clear grasp of the problem and develop questions that reflect that clarity. Open-ended questions are not the same as unclear questions. The focus group discussion is of limited value unless the participants truly understand what they are being asked. Often, the lack of clarity is due to a lack of conceptual rigor by the researcher. Other times, the lack of clarity is just illustrative of our culture, in which we talk about ambiguous concepts such as diversity, equity, satisfaction, leadership, etc., without really defining what we are talking about.

Note the Discussion on Clarity in Chapter 1: "Guiding Principles of Asking Questions"

Cultural Constraints

Culture greatly influences what kinds of questions are appropriate in a focus group. Mainstream American culture, often characterized as forthright and candid, is not a workable model for other cultures around the world. Questions that may be effective in white, middle-class American focus groups would be considered rude, inappropriate, or unethical in other focus groups. In addition, the appropriateness of a question is greatly influenced by contextual factors, such as why the research is needed, who will be using the results, and who is asking the questions.

Recently, in focus groups on an Indian reservation, the questions were adapted to fit into the traditional conversational patterns of local residents. In this tribe, it was customary for the elders, who were not necessarily the oldest people present, to speak last—after others had shared their opinions. Furthermore, it was not appropriate to talk after the elders had spoken. As a result, the researchers adapted the questions and process, adding questions specifically for the elders who, in turn, provided summaries to particular questions.

Language Constraints

Over the past decade, increasing numbers of focus groups throughout the United States have been conducted in languages other than English. Public and nonprofit organizations began conducting focus groups in other languages as researchers sought clues on developing community strengths, solving community problems, and developing culturally appropriate interventions. Market researchers began conducting non-English focus groups due to the increasing market share of these groups. Most market research groups are conducted for consumer products; at present, one of the faster growth areas is with Spanish-speaking focus groups.

One primary constraint in conducting focus groups is that the moderator must understand the language. Conducting focus groups through an interpreter is not only difficult and tedious, but also of questionable research value. Asking participants to speak in a language other than their first language can make participants uncomfortable and severely limit discussion because they may lack the words that best express their views. A better strategy is to conduct groups in the first language of participants with a moderator fluent in both that language and English.

Sometimes, when translating a question into another language, the meaning gets changed. To prevent this, you might consider using "back translations" of the questions by a second translator. The English questions are translated into the target language by the first translator. These are then given to a second translator, who is asked to translate them back into English. This translation is then compared with the original question. This process helps ensure clarity and accuracy of the questions.

9

Changing Questions
The Importance of Consistency

When doing a series of focus groups, a concern that often arises is the need for consistency among groups. Should questions remain constant throughout a series of focus groups? Should questions be the same across differing groups of participants?

Usually Questions Are Not Changed

The general rule of thumb is to maintain as much consistency as possible throughout the series of focus groups, for it is in comparison and contrast that themes and patterns emerge from the data. Information obtained from a single focus group can yield interesting and, at times, helpful insights, but the researcher just does not know if similar findings would occur in another group. In analysis, the researcher strives for theoretical saturation, which is only possible with consistency of questioning.

BACKGROUND

**What Is
Theoretical
Saturation?**

Theoretical saturation is a process of adding additional cases (or focus groups) until you have reduced variation and uncovered the range of experiences. You have essentially discovered what there is to discover. The actual number is unimportant, but each case should aid the researcher. When additional interviews or observations do not yield new insights, the researcher has reached the point of "theoretical saturation." Sampling until you have reached theoretical saturation comes from Glaser and Strauss (1967, pp. 61-62, 111-112).

Using Parallel and Similar Questions

Parallel questions are those deemed to be equivalent. The concept is the same, but the words are different. Parallel questions are helpful for the moderator to use when participants do not understand the original question. Instead of asking the same question in the very same words, which just frustrates participants, the moderator asks the question in a parallel format. Sometimes, the moderator repeats the question using a parallel form, such as when the moderator suspects that more could be said about a particular topic. Other times, when a research team of moderators is going out to different groups or communities, the parallel construction clearly communicates the question's intent across cultures, ages, educational levels, and so on. Parallel questions tend to be used more frequently in focus groups where the researcher's education, occupation, or background is different from that of the participants.

EXAMPLE

Parallel Questions

- *"What prevents youth from using drugs?" (is PARALLEL to) "What keeps kids away from drugs?"*
- *"What role did others have in your success?" (is PARALLEL to) "How did others help you succeed?"*
- *"What would get you to participate in this program?" (is PARALLEL to) "Under what conditions would you get involved?*
- *"What would you want to know?" (is PARALLEL to) "What kind of information would you like to get?"*
- *"What would entice you to come back for more?" (is PARALLEL to) "What would keep you interested?"*
- *"What does the word violence mean to you?" (is PARALLEL to) "What is your definition of violence?"*

A slight variation is what we call the similar question. The similar question is one that is similar in concept but is asked differently with differing participants. This type of question is helpful when you are comparing and contrasting the same concept with differing audiences.

In a drug prevention study, teens and adults were asked similar questions:

- *Teen:* "What is the most pressing problem you face today?"
- *Adult:* "What is the most pressing problem faced by teens today?"
- *Teen:* "What keeps you from using drugs?"
- *Adult:* "What keeps youth from using drugs?"

EXAMPLE

Similar Questions

Circumstances When Questions Might Change

Occasionally, it is wise to change or eliminate a question in a focus group interview. Here are three circumstances when this should be considered.

Change the question if it clearly doesn't work. This is often spotted in one of the first focus groups. There are three clues that a question doesn't work: when there is silence and no one answers the question; when participants tell you that they don't understand the question; and when participants talk but are not answering the question. This third condition is often difficult for novice moderators to spot because they judge success by the amount of discussion. If the moderator recognizes that the participants are off the topic, he or she should ask the question again. The test is if the discussion shows that participants have really understood the question. Here's an example of when a question just didn't work: We asked veterans, "Think back to when you were first diagnosed with depression. How helpful were the tests you received?" The veterans couldn't remember what tests they had received, and we dropped the question.

Change the question if saturation has occurred. In many studies, theoretical saturation occurs somewhere between 3 and 12 focus groups. When conducting a sizable number of focus groups, there is little to gain by continuing to ask questions when the responses are predictable. There is considerably more to gain by changing questions to build on what you have learned in the earlier groups. Essentially, the researcher is learning nothing new after saturation has occurred. Here's an example of a change due to saturation. In the same study with veterans, we asked veterans what they thought of having peer counselors—counselors who had been through similar experiences. After about six groups, the answer to this was clear and consistent, so we dropped the question and added another.

BACKGROUND

Changing Questions Based on Analysis

A critical difference between qualitative and quantitative studies is the timing of analysis. In focus group interviews, analysis begins with the first focus group and continues until after the final focus group. Analysis occurs simultaneously with data collection. In contrast, the analysis in quantitative studies begins after all data (often surveys) have been collected. It is possible to conduct focus group analysis by waiting until the end of all focus groups, but the researcher misses the opportunity to use analysis feedback in later focus group interviews or to refine the questions. One of the major benefits of research using multiple focus groups is the opportunity to fine-tune questions, bring questions to another level, and solicit participant interpretation of earlier findings.

Change the question if past responses lead you to another level. When conducting a series of focus groups, the researcher may find that ideas or concepts discovered in early focus groups change the way the problem is envisioned. When this occurs, the researchers may want to modify the questions to reflect the current reality. For example, in a recent study on future directions for a university, people were asked about areas that the university should emphasize. One of those that emerged was the need for greater diversity. Unfortunately, this concept was not followed up in later focus groups, and much is still unknown about the need for diversity. How was diversity defined? What does diversity mean to participants? Do differing audiences agree or disagree? What shapes their opinion of the need for diversity? What would be credible examples of diversity within the university? All of these questions and more could have been explored in subsequent focus groups, thereby raising the level of understanding on this important topic.

10

Pilot Testing and Reviewing the Plan

Overview

Pilot Test Questions
Reviewing the Focus Group Plan

Pilot testing of focus group questions is difficult. Although pilot testing is a cardinal rule of research, it presents special problems with focus groups. More than other forms of social science research, the questions used in a focus group interview are hard to separate from the environment of the focus group. If the focus group fails, how do you know that the cause was the questions and not the moderator, the room, the recruiting, or a host of other factors? A strategy to consider is to separate the pilot testing of questions from the pilot testing or reviewing of the focus group plan.

The true pilot test is the first focus group with participants. As one veteran moderator said, "Do the first focus group. If it works, it's your first group. If it doesn't, it was a pilot test." Unfortunately, this strategy can be costly and time-consuming, and better ways are available. We suggest the following procedures.

KEY POINT

Separate Pilot Testing of Questions From Reviewing of Focus Group Plan

Pilot Test Questions

With Research Team Members

The first and easiest strategy is for researchers to try the questions on other researchers or staff who are familiar with the program or activity. It's best if the questions aren't read but asked conversationally. The first researcher asks the question, and the second researcher attempts to answer. With this exercise, several aspects are tested at once. One is the ease with which the question can be asked, and another is the nature of the answer.

First, let's consider the question. Does it seem awkward when asked orally? Do the words flow smoothly? Does it sound conversational? By tone and inflection, the moderator places emphasis on certain key words in the question. Is this emphasis correct?

Second, let's consider the responses. Do responses occur relatively quickly? Are questions misinterpreted? Do responses shed light on the topic of examination in the focus group study? This part of the exercise also helps in analysis because it identifies expected responses.

With Experts

Another way to pilot test questions is to submit the questions to a focus group expert. This is occasionally helpful, but it is difficult for the expert because each set of questions is driven by context, which is often unknown to the expert. Nevertheless, experts do bring a wealth of experience and can offer insights based on their experiences with similar questions. When experts have been asked to review focus group questions, especially those developed by novices, several common problems often emerge. These include too many questions, questions that are written in the researcher's language rather than the participant's language, excessive complexity, and inaccurate assumptions about cause and effect.

With Potential Participants and Nonresearchers

Seek feedback from potential participants and other nonresearchers. The research team does this pilot testing by asking questions of individuals who are not familiar with the study but represent a lay perspective. This pilot testing is often done with people who meet the specifications for being in the focus group. When this is not practical, beneficial results can often be obtained from other nonresearchers, such as family members, friends, acquaintances, and others. This pilot testing need not occur in group situations; valuable results have been obtained from one-to-one discussions.

Here's the beginning part of a coffee shop conversation: "We're doing a study on community needs that is sponsored by the University. We're planning to conduct interviews with people here in town, and I'd like your advice on the questions. Would you listen to the questions, give your answers, and then tell me your opinions on the questions? It'll only take a few minutes. Should we try it?"

One of the easiest ways to do this pilot testing with potential participants is to invite one or two people like the potential participants to lunch and ask their advice on the questions as well as on logistics, recruitment strategies, and other factors pertaining to the focus group.

Reviewing the Focus Group Plan

You may wish to review the entire focus group plan. This occurs when the researchers consider more than just the questions. The selection process, the recruitment strategies, the invitation protocol, the introduction to the focus group, and the skills of the moderator are all part of the equation.

With Research Team Members

The focus group is reviewed by dividing the overall process into discrete steps. By taking one step at a time, the research team reviews the protocol for effectiveness, efficiency, and practicality. How are participants located and then invited to the focus group? Do recruitment procedures meet the recommended protocol, or have the proposed strategies been successful in the past with similar audiences? Other factors to consider are the physical facilities, the content of advance information given to participants, and the focus group introduction given by the moderator at the beginning of the discussion.

With Experts

The review with experts involves sharing protocol and documents, as well as demonstrating the introduction to the focus group and the questions. This is often a valuable investment because it enables the expert to see the entire design of the study.

With Participants

At the end of the focus group, the moderator asks the participants for comments about the discussion, for example, "This is the first of our discussions. We're planning to hold several more over the coming weeks. What advice do you have for us?"

If major changes are made in the questions or moderator procedures, then the results of the first focus group are set aside and not used in later analysis. If, however, there are no major changes, the first "pilot" discussion is included in later analysis.

Part III

Questions That
Engage Participants

Up to now, we've relied almost exclusively on questions that only required people to talk. We will now expand our options to include questions that ask people to do something, to become engaged, or to become more actively involved. There are several benefits to creating activities and experiences that get people to write, draw, speak, debate, and so on. Participants will not only have fun, but they will also become engaged in a different way that taps into a different part of the brain or heart. Out of these experiences emerges useful information that can be helpful in your study.

11

Listing, Rating, and Choosing Questions

Questions can be fun. Too often we get into a rut, but with a little help, our questions can be both enjoyable and productive. The first category that we will examine is questions that engage people in listing, rating, and choosing from among alternatives. Much can be learned from these activities because they provide a different way of offering information. Some participants are comfortable and effective in offering immediate verbal responses, but others are more reflective and need extra minutes for thought or a chance to write down or sketch out their ideas. As a result, these activity-oriented questions offer special benefits, and they are particularly effective midway through the focus group interview. Let's examine some possible strategies.

Listing Things

Perhaps the easiest strategy is to make a list. This is often done with a flip chart or chalkboard so participants can remember what has already been said. There are several ways that the list can be prepared. One way is to have participants verbally offer ideas while the moderator or assistant moderator records these on the flip chart. Another way is to give participants several minutes to record their individual lists on paper provided to them and then tabulate results. The lists can be read aloud by the participants, read by the moderator, or sorted and read by the assistant moderator. This listing process helps identify duplicate items. The listing process also affords the participants a few moments to reflect before they offer an answer.

EXAMPLE

Listing Things

- *"Think back to when you had awful service. What makes customer service terrible? Write your answers on a piece of paper. In a moment, we'll share these with each other."*

- *"What are three things you think of when you purchase soap? Take a moment and write these down on a piece of paper. When you're finished, we'll share these with each other."*

- *"On the paper in front of you, jot down three characteristics of successful youth workers."*

Rating Using a Predetermined Scale

This predetermined scale is developed before the focus group by the research team. It may be borrowed from some previous study, be based on past experiences with the topic, or grow out of theoretical principles. Both the criteria and the response choices are predetermined and placed in a format easy for focus group participants to use. The rating scale should be simple, and participants should be able to complete it within a few minutes. Consequently, there is a limit to the number of items that can be listed on a rating scale.

Most frequently, the exercise involves about five to ten criteria and offers a rating scale with a range of numbers, adjectives, or both. When numbers are used, the scale might consist of a straightforward range of three, four, five, or ten points. Offer a scale and anchor the ends of the scale with adjectives (high and low, poor and excellent, positive and negative). For example, "We're going to use a four-point scale with one being poor and four being excellent. Use this scale and rate each characteristic of the proposed program." When finished, the moderator can ask that the rating scales be handed in for quick calculation or just be announced orally by each participant. Following quick tabulation, the group discusses the meaning of the ratings. Be careful about the pressure for conformity, because in some situations, participants will adjust their answers based on what other participants have said. To counteract this tendency and avoid last-minute shifting of responses, it is desirable to have participants actually write down, circle, or check off their response choices. This deliberate act helps establish the participants' commitment to their answers.

When adjectives are used, it is best to use commonly accepted words instead of creating new categories. Note the example below of adjective-based rating scales that are in common use.

Examples of Adjective Rating Scales

excellent	strongly agree	very important
good	agree	somewhat important
fair	neutral	slightly important
poor	disagree	not important
	strongly disagree	

very helpful	to a great extent	very satisfied
fairly helpful	to a moderate extent	somewhat satisfied
slightly helpful	to a slight extent	undecided
no help at all	not at all	somewhat dissatisfied
		very dissatisfied

EXAMPLE

Adjective-Based Rating Scales

Yet another scale could be a semantic differential with participants offering ratings on the current status and the desired, or hoped for, status. The semantic differential presents a series of spaces with opposite adjectives anchoring each end of the scale. Ask participants to place a check mark in the space that best represents their point of view.

We used a semantic differential scale in a study of higher education within a community. We asked participants to rate higher education in their community as it is now and as it should be. Our concern was not their scores but the gaps, or differences, between the status quo and how they would like the situation to be. After participants completed their scoring, we asked them all to tell us the categories where their differences were the greatest. "Where is the greatest gap in your scores between what 'is now' compared with what 'should be'?" These categories then became the areas that we discussed in greater detail.

EXAMPLE

Semantic Differential Scale

Listed below are words that might describe higher education in the community. Note that the words on the same line have opposite meanings. Place a check mark in one of the five spaces that represents how you feel about higher education in the community NOW. Then do the rating below for how you feel higher education in the community SHOULD BE in the future.

Higher Education in Our Community IS NOW?					
Convenient					Inconvenient
Fragmented					Coordinated
Customer-focused					Not customer-focused
High quality					Inferior quality
Concerned teachers					Indifferent teachers
Colleges work together					Colleges work independently

Higher Education in Our Community SHOULD BE?					
Convenient					Inconvenient
Fragmented					Coordinated
Customer-focused					Not customer-focused
High quality					Inferior quality
Concerned teachers					Indifferent teachers
Colleges work together					Colleges work independently

The purpose of the rating scale is *not* to achieve statistical precision but to foster discussion in the focus group. The numbers or adjectives are intended to get focus group participants to think about the concept, offer a judgment, share it with others, and then discuss the concept. It's not unusual for participants to want to change their ratings after discussion. These rating scales exist to promote discussion, and in fact, without discussion it would be an impractical way to collect survey information.

Sometimes, researchers ask if they can tabulate the scores and use the results in the focus group report. There is nothing wrong with this as long as the researcher and those using the results know that these scores reflect small samples that are not intended to represent a population. The emphasis, however, should not be on average scores but on the resulting discussion. Among other things, here are some questions that the researchers may want to consider: Were there areas of agreement among participants? Were there special conditions or circumstances that influenced a particular rating? Did participants seem surprised by others' scores? Were criteria missing from the list? Did participants show interest in changing their scores after discussion? What arguments prompted these changes? These and other questions are topics that help researchers understand participants' perspectives.

Moderators might consider using some of these follow-up questions after the discussion:

- Where do we agree? (In what areas do we agree?)
- Are there differences of opinion in our group?
- Did anything surprise you?
- Would you change any of your scores now, after you've listened to others?

Rating Using a Self-Determined Scale

The self-determined scale is one developed completely by partici-pants in the focus group. Often, participants develop criteria for scales, and sometimes, they also develop response scales. It's important to remember the purpose of these scales. These scales exist not to provide precise ratings of phenomena but to stimulate and foster later discussion among participants.

The advantage of these self-developed scales is that they truly represent the spirit of an open-ended question. These questions allow participants to identify the criteria, from their personal perspectives, and to identify a level of scoring that reflects their reality. The disadvantage of self-developed scales is the difficulty, or even impossibility, of aggregating or effectively summarizing within a group or across groups.

Suppose we are interested in how customers rate a local restaurant. We could use a scale often used by restaurants, and if we did so, we could compare results with previous findings. But the predetermined scale might also miss some critical elements of customer concern. Most often, these rating forms ask about quality of food, quantity of food, speed of service, friendliness of service, etc. Suppose, however, that areas of greater concern to customers are parking lot congestion, traffic, food prices, pres-ence or absence of smoking areas, noisiness, or some other concern unanticipated by those developing the criteria. Weigh the pros and cons of a preestablished scale versus one developed by participants. The advantage of using criteria and a scale devel-oped by all the participants is that you get closer to their reality.

Do they, for example, have a dichotomous, two-point scale, such as acceptable and unacceptable? Or do they see a particular concern as a continuum, and if so, what are the anchor points and the points in the middle?

Essentially, you have three viable choices if you are interested in using a self-determined rating scale. You can ask all participants to identify their own criteria and use an established response scale. You can ask participants to develop both the criteria and their own response scale. Or, you can invite the group to develop the criteria and use a response scale established by the researcher. There are advantages and disadvantages of each, as described in the following examples.

EXAMPLE

Options With a Self-Determined Rating Scale

When using a self-determined rating scale, these options are possible:

- *Participants develop criteria and use established response scale.*

  Assessment: *Relatively quick and offers each individual the chance to select his or her own criteria. A limitation is that the response scale may not adequately depict how participants envision the topic.*
  Example used with students in a high school: *"We'd like you to grade the school. You're familiar with grades, A, B, C, D, and F, that are received for school subjects such as language arts, history, and algebra. We want you to grade the school, but you get to pick the subjects or the areas to grade. Pick subjects or things that are important to you. It could be something about people, the building, activities, or anything connected with the school. Pick subjects and give each subject a grade from A to F."*

- *Participants develop both criteria and response scale.*

  Assessment: *Offers greatest freedom to participants, but the task is sometimes too difficult for participants to understand. Also, the results are difficult to analyze. Comparison and aggregation are usually impossible.*
  Example used in a community: *"We want to find out about community needs. Think for a moment about various people here in our community and their needs. Pick five needs, and for each, indicate its level of importance. You can use any rating scale you want."*

- *Participants develop criteria as a group and use a response scale developed by the researcher..*

  Assessment: *This strategy takes time to identify the criteria that are developed by participants, often by listing and voting. Participants then use a scale developed by the researchers to rate criteria. The disadvantage is that this strategy can be time-consuming.*
  Example used in an organization: *"We want to identify areas that need attention in our unit. Make a list of those things that you feel are important to do in our unit. When we're finished, we'll share these with each other and list them on a flip chart. After they're shared, we'll ask you to rate the importance of each suggestion on a four-point scale."*

Another form of rating responses in focus groups is the use of handheld electronic devices incorporating a keypad or rheostat and connected to a computer. Participants are asked to observe, listen, taste, or experience something and then express their rating with the handheld device. The moderator can immediately tabulate responses and use these results in later discussion or can move on to additional items. The advantage of these systems is that they can offer immediate tabulation and anonymity. Disadvantages include cost, the novelty of the device, and the complexity of high tech. There is not much that these systems offer that cannot be done with paper and pencil at a fraction of the cost.

Choosing Among Alternatives

Choosing among alternatives is very popular in focus group interviews. Participants are offered several choices, usually at least three and no more than five. The participants are asked to look over the alternatives, talk about the advantages and disadvantages of each, and select the one that they like the best, believe is most appropriate, or fits the description. In addition to making the selection and announcing the choice, the participants also offer a reason for why they decided the way they did. This strategy is often used in selecting from among visual displays, advertising layouts, potential promotional materials, or even program options. We've used this strategy in identifying options for higher education in a community, delivering social service programs, and offering nonformal education. In some situations, the participants were given short descriptions to read. In others, participants watched short videos or reviewed materials or mock-ups. Participants were allowed to ask questions about each option, after which they were to select the one they most preferred.

Arranging Categories—Conceptual Mapping

Suppose a service agency wants to discover how potential customers see the agency. One way to do this is to incorporate a process called conceptual mapping into the focus group. This exercise allows each participant to describe the agency in relation to similar organizations, using the participant's classification system. The exercise begins when participants are given a sheet of paper showing a box divided into four quadrants. On the sheet, they are are asked to list all organizations that perform similar services, grouping the ones that they consider to be similar into the same cells. They need not use all four quadrants, and if more are needed, they can be added.

The moderator gives the participants about 5 minutes to complete the exercise. When the exercise is completed, the moderator asks the participants, one at a time, to share their results. The moderator asks each participant to explain the categories chosen. When all have shared results, the moderator can pursue additional discussion of the commonalities and differences between various cells. In essence, the participants develop a classification system that describes similar or different items based on categories they have developed. An individual may categorize the choices in a variety of ways: by cost, convenience, size of operation, availability, or a host of other means. The greater insight comes from the discussion as the moderator listens to the rationale for the classification.

The conceptual mapping strategy makes a critical assumption. It assumes that participants are sufficiently familiar with the choices to be able to recall what they are and are able to identify differences among the alternatives. If the topic is specific and tangible, such as toothpaste, breakfast cereals, or automobiles, then the participants can often launch right into the exercise. In other cases, the topic may be abstract, relating to programs, opportunities, or organizations that have multiple functions. In these cases, the moderator might begin the exercise by listing on a flip chart all possible choices that the participants can think of before the choices are classified. If some are unfamiliar with the choices, the moderator might invite brief descriptions.

Sorting Pictures

The picture sort resembles the collage discussed in Chapter 12 of this volume. It begins with a stack of pictures from magazines, such as a stack of pictures of women, men, or teens. The pictures depict people doing a variety of things. The moderator asks the participants to sort through the pictures and pick out those that match certain characteristics. For example, "Look through these pictures and pick out the people who would participate in community education"; "Here are some pictures of women. Sort the pictures into two categories. One category is the women who would likely breast-feed their child, and the second category is those who would likely bottle-feed their child." After the sorting exercise, the moderator might ask participants what the pictures had in common and how they came to be selected.

12

Projective Questions

Overview

Completing a Sentence
Developing a Collage
Drawing a Picture
Creating Analogies
Creating Families
Using Personification
Using Fantasy and Daydreams
Analysis of Projective Questions

Sometimes participants feel that their answers may not be correct—politically, socially, or intellectually. At other times, the answer cannot be shared because it is below a level of articulation. Although participants may have feelings about the topic, they cannot express them in words. Consider projective questioning techniques in these situations, because they reduce the seriousness of the topic and tap into different ways of thinking.

Projective techniques work because they circumvent several possible barriers to expression. For example, sometimes we are unable to express attitudes because our ideas are not yet clearly formed. The projective strategy makes the task easier because it shifts the topic of inquiry to something that is seemingly easier and simpler. Another barrier is the perceived social acceptability of our answers. We worry that others might not like what we say, so we consciously monitor our comments. In the focus group, this problem is minimized by the permissive sanctioning of the moderator and the perceived group support for sharing alternative views. Still another barrier is the tendency to limit our answers to only one way of thinking, such as right-brain or left-brain responses, instead of tapping into multiple domains. Projective techniques allow participants to express themselves in multiple ways.

Projective techniques seek information on a particular topic by asking about a different and often easier topic. After discussion of the secondary topic, the moderator asks participants to make links back to the primary topic.

Completing a Sentence

In sentence completion exercises, the sentences are prepared in advance and are printed on a piece of paper. Participants are given a few minutes to complete the sentences, and then results are shared. When sharing results, the moderator might read the first question and then go around the table asking each person to tell how he or she answered that question. When finished, the moderator might ask participants for their comments or observations on what was said. Alternatively, the moderator might ask them what they saw to be similar or different among the responses. The sentence completion exercise has the benefit of allowing participants a few moments to reflect before developing their responses.

For an Overview of Projective Techniques, See Branthwaite and Lunn, "Projective Techniques in Social and Market Research"

EXAMPLE

Sentence Completion

- *When I first found out that my cholesterol was high, I felt* _____ _____ _____

- *Now, as I think about the changes I made in my diet, what really helped me was* _____ _____

- *What got in the way of my progress was* _____ _____ _____

- *I was surprised that* _____ _____ _____

- *One problem with this program is* _____ _____ _____

Developing a Collage

In a focus group, the collage is a display prepared and presented by participants. The display has a theme or a topic of interest, which is assigned by the moderator. Participants are given access to materials that they may wish to include in their collage. The materials can be magazines or newspapers, promotional flyers or brochures, and files of pictures or advertisements.

The moderator usually divides the focus group into two or three smaller teams, each with two to four participants. The teams work independently for 15 to 30 minutes as they prepare their displays. Participants add their own words or draw their own pictures if they wish. When time is up, the total group reassembles, and each team presents its work for group comments and feedback.

- *Community education*

  Suppose community education wanted to get a profile of how residents view their services. Armed with stacks of magazines, paste or tape, and large sheets of paper, the moderator asks participants to illustrate answers to questions in their displays. The questions asked are, "What kind of person participates in community education in our schools?" "What kind of person doesn't participate?" "What are the interests and hobbies of residents in our community?"

- *Healthy eating for preteens*

  A focus group with preteens seeks to discover persuasive strategies for healthy eating. After a few preliminary questions, the young people are divided into teams, given stacks of newspapers and magazines, and asked to prepare a display reflecting responses to three questions:

    1. What is healthy eating?
    2. What gets in the way of healthy eating?
    3. What's the benefit of healthy eating?

- *Teen smoking prevention*

  A focus group of teens is divided into two teams. Each team is assigned a question and asked to develop a collage. One team is asked to describe kids who smoke. The second team is asked to describe kids who don't smoke. After presenting results, the moderator asks the whole group what has been learned.

EXAMPLE

Developing a Collage

Drawing a Picture

Each focus group participant is given a blank piece of paper and a pencil. The participants are then asked to draw a picture that might offer some insights on behavior or attitudes. Use stick figures for those who are anxious about the difficulty of drawing people.

EXAMPLE

Drawing Pictures

- *"We want you to draw someone who uses the youth center. Give the people names and ages and tell where they live. Tell us where they go to school and what their hobbies are. Draw a picture of your person standing at the door of the youth center after having spent the evening there. This person is holding something and saying something. Draw something in the hand, and write down what the person is saying."*

- *"We are studying customer satisfaction. Draw a picture of a happy customer and write down what that person is saying. Then draw a picture of a disappointed customer and write down what that person is saying."*

- *"Draw a picture of good employee morale."*

- *"Draw a picture of an employee. Draw an arrow to his or her mouth, and write down what this person says about our organization. Draw an arrow to the head, and write down what he or she thinks about the organization. Then draw an arrow to the heart, and write down what he or she feels about the organization."*

After all participants have drawn their pictures, they are asked to hold the drawings up for others to see and then describe them. When the group is finished sharing, the moderator might ask the group what they saw in the different approaches. What was similar? What was different?

As with all these participatory exercises, the benefit is in the discussion that follows the drawing of the pictures. The pictures are merely the stimulus that helps participants collect their thoughts and explain how they see a concept or idea.

Creating Analogies

With the analogy, the moderator asks how the target topic is like another topic. Select categories that are familiar to participants. Some categories are used often, such as animals or automobiles, but whatever the categories, they need to be familiar to participants. These could involve such things as workshop tools, restaurants, department stores, things found in the kitchen, flowers, trees, or insects. You might follow up with a question on what the participants see in common (or as different) between the various analogies. At times, the interpretation of results can be risky, and the moderator should invite participants to explain their analogies.

- *"Suppose that this agency was a restaurant. What sort of place would it be and what would it be like?"*
- *"If this organization were a chair, what kind of chair would it be and how would it feel?"*
- *"Think about the people you've met in our organization. If they were animals*, what type of animal would they be?" THEN: "Why did you pick that animal?"*

  * Instead of animals, you might use colors, something found around the home, a TV program, etc.

EXAMPLE

Analogy Projective Technique

Creating Families

Creating families is a task used to uncover relationships between the target category and other categories. How does this topic fit in a category? What others fit into the same category? Families have some connections and relationships. They may look, act, or function in similar ways. They have both ancestors and offspring. The family analogy can lead to interesting relationships, such as identifying grandparents or children, black sheep, the favorite child, the crazy aunt, and so forth. This exercise also lends itself to several follow-up questions about the family analogy. What makes a group of items a family? What doesn't make it a family? How would you describe this family? What strengths does this family have? What's needed to improve this family?

- *"Suppose that this program was a family. What other programs would be in the same family?"*
- *"Suppose that all (educational, human service, etc.) agencies in our community are family members. How would you describe this family?"*

EXAMPLE

Family Projective Technique

Using Personification

With personification, the participants are asked how the target topic is like a person, and what kind of person it would be. The moderator asks for a description of personal attributes. In effect, an inanimate object (organization, program, option, demonstration project) is brought to life, and the respondent is asked to tell how it looks and behaves. Personification works because it interrupts the usual thinking pattern and creates a different domain where new light is shed on the object of attention. Once the object is described in personal (or animal) terms, ask follow-up questions on gender, age, occupation, personality qualities, and so on. Watch for how certain human differences may influence the description.

EXAMPLE

**Personification
Projective
Technique**

- *"Suppose that your organization is a person; tell me what this person would be like."*
- *"If community education were a person, how would you describe that person?"*
- *"Three foundations are suddenly changed into people. They are the Kellogg Foundation, the Northwest Area Foundation, and the McKnight Foundation. They are now people, and you're at a social gathering with these three people. What are they like?"*

Using Fantasy and Daydreams

Occasionally, moderators will ask participants to describe fantasies and daydreams in order to surface characteristics or features that are important to the study. The challenge for the moderator is to establish the timing of the experience so that participants are ready for the exercise. For example, after participants have talked about the pros and cons of an alternative, the moderator might tell participants that there is a magic wand, hat, or device that allows them to make their fantasy come true. The moderator passes around the wand or hat, and as each participant holds the wand or puts on the hat, each one also shares a fantasy. Alternatively, participants might be asked to close their eyes and imagine that they are on a special journey in a faraway land. Along the way, they discover a special box that holds answers to great problems and difficulties that people have. They open the box and find the answer to the problem. What is in the box?

The moderator begins the experience by changing the pace of the group discussion. Up to this point, participants are answering questions and conversing with others. Now, the moderator changes the mood of the conversation, perhaps by asking for a moment of silence, by using music to create a period of relaxation, or by presenting descriptive imagery. For example, a moderator was seeking creative suggestions for displays at a nutrition carnival and asked participants to close their eyes, listen to the carnival music, and imagine themselves at the carnival. This was a special carnival that helped people to learn and use nutritious diets. The participants were asked to describe what they saw.

EXAMPLE

Fantasy and Daydreams

- *"Here is a magic wand. I shall pass it around the table, and when you receive it, you will give your magical solution to the problem. By waving the wand, your solution will come true. Take the wand, and tell us your solution."*

- *"Close your eyes for a moment. Imagine that you have been cryogenically frozen. You are completely OK, except that you wake up 20 years in the future. This is an ideal future. What's the future like? What is your organization doing to help people?"*

- *"Now I would like you to daydream for a bit. Close your eyes for a moment, and I will describe a situation. Then, in a moment, I'll ask you to open your eyes and tell me what you saw. You are on a special journey in a place far away. You're on a quest to find a treasure box left for you by someone from your past whom you greatly respect. It takes some effort and time to arrive at this special place. When you arrive, you locate the box. What does it look like? What does it smell like? What does it feel like? You've been told that this box contains just what your organization needs at this time. You open the box, and you find the answer. Open your eyes now, and take a few minutes to write down, or draw, what you found. Then, in a moment, we'll ask you to tell us about it."*

- *"You are a student who has just received great help from the university. You are absolutely delighted with the help you've received. Tell us about what happened to you."*

Analysis of Projective Questions

Analysis of projective results is admittedly subjective, and we encourage a two-part strategy that involves both participant assistance and multiple data sources. In clinical settings, especially those involving individual interviews, there are accepted and standard interpretations for projective tests. The focus group use of projective questions, however, is different, in that it takes place in a practical, real-life environment and involves a small group instead of individuals. Therefore, the analysis ought to grow out of this environment.

We suggest that you begin by asking participants what their answers mean. It is important for the participants to tell the researcher where to place attention. Interpretation of the projective question is largely a task for the participant, but with careful yet skillful guidance from the researcher. Over a series of focus groups, a pattern emerges that allows a more confident analysis.

The second stage of analysis uses multiple sources of information. Projective techniques are but one facet of reality that must be blended with other facets for the total impression. The proportions of the mix and the weight placed on projective questions are in the hands of the researcher and indeed require a judgment.

13

Group Activities

Overview

Developing a Campaign
Role Playing
Mini-Team Debate

Developing a Campaign

Recently, several youth focus group studies have used a "campaign" questioning strategy. The session begins with the moderator asking questions of the youth about campaigns: "What is a campaign?" "Tell us about where you've seen campaigns?" "What happens in a campaign?" "What are the things that make up a campaign?" During this first part, the young people typically talk about political campaigns and sometimes campaigns for schools, teams, or local causes. Campaigns have slogans, speakers, banners, songs, balloons, and celebrities. The moderator then asks the participants to develop a campaign that will get other young people to do something—perhaps eat better foods, live a healthier lifestyle, or avoid drugs and alcohol. The campaign is aimed at other kids. Those in the focus group plan the strategy, complete with slogans, speakers, music, and anything else needed to be effective. There is a supply of materials, like markers and colored paper, for the kids to use in developing their campaign. If the group is large, the moderator might divide it into two small groups of three to five participants to work for 45 minutes to an hour and then reassemble and share results. Kids then share their campaigns and talk about what they like best about each campaign.

This strategy works well with youth because it allows them to be active, to use their expertise, and to have fun. You can get creative with this. One researcher provided T-shirts and caps to the kids, so they could identify themselves as their own marketing group. The researcher learns which strategies the target audience finds to be effective. This campaign strategy also works with adults in promoting social issues, community activities, wellness campaigns, and a host of other efforts.

Role Playing

In role playing, the focus group participants are asked to pretend that they are in a particular situation and then offer workable strategies and solutions. Role playing is helpful in finding out about complex human interactions through demonstrations. Usually, the role playing takes place with one or two participants playing the roles with the remaining focus group participants observing the interaction and later, after it is finished, offering reactions.

The unique advantage of role playing is that it places people as close as possible to a situation of interest. This is an experience in which the researcher has the opportunity for observation with the added benefit of feedback from a jury. Role playing works particularly well in several situations. Sometimes, participants cannot effectively describe actions or behaviors in an abstract sense, but they can demonstrate how they are done.

When the role playing is completed—and it usually lasts only a few minutes—the remaining focus group participants are asked for their observations: "What did you think?" "Was this realistic?" "Would anyone else like to try it?"

EXAMPLE

Role Playing

- *Handling customer service*

  "Dorothy, perhaps you could show us how you would handle complaints about poor service. Suppose that you now work for an airline company. You are the person behind the counter, and Margaret is the customer who's upset about the way she's been treated. Margaret, would you begin by making the complaint to Dorothy that you just described to us in the group? Then, Dorothy, we'd like you to respond to Margaret's concerns in the way you think complaints in the airline industry should be handled."

- *Encouraging faculty outreach effort*

  "We've been talking about how to convince faculty at the university to take on nonpaid outreach efforts in the community. Several of you had some thoughts about what would be persuasive to colleagues. John, I'd like to ask you to have a conversation with Mary. Mary is a colleague in your department, and she's been reluctant to get involved in community outreach efforts. Mary, as the reluctant colleague, your task is to offer arguments or opinions that might be held by other faculty. The rest of us will watch and listen."

- *Talking to kids about drug and alcohol use*

  "OK, we've talked about how parents have difficulty in talking to teens about drugs and alcohol. Let's reverse the situation. We'd like to see how you would do it. Jane, you are now a parent of a teenager, and you really don't want your daughter to use drugs or alcohol. Jane, you get to pick out the best time and place for the conversation. Tell us where and when it is. Then pretend that Betty is your daughter. What would you say to Betty, your daughter? Betty, you have a chance to respond. Assume Jane is your mother."

Mini-Team Debate

The mini-team debate is a variation on role playing, in that participants are assigned a topic and are expected to present the best case or argument for a particular point of view. Those listening to the presentation are expected to respond and present the opposing point of view.

The exercise begins by having the moderator divide the focus group participants into several teams. Typically two to four people form a team. Perhaps the most often used format consists of two teams, one to present the case and the second to respond. (A variation is to have three or more teams and have a "daisy chain" process with each team first responding to the best argument of the previous team, followed by presenting their best argument to the next team.)

The teams are given a short time (about 3 to 5 minutes) to discuss their best arguments or what the best arguments might be from the opposing team and how they might counter these arguments. Mini-team debates can be used on such topics as the use of seat belts, new directions for an organization, possible responses to a persistent bureaucratic problem, or teenage use of alcohol.

Appendix
Examples of Questions

Here are some examples of questions used in focus group studies. Feel free to look over these examples and borrow words, phrases, or entire questions. These focus groups were conducted for a variety of topics, ranging from needs assessments to organizational development and evaluation.

Training Needs of Dentists

1. Tell us your name, where you practice, and what you enjoy doing the most when you're not practicing dentistry.
2. We are here to talk about continuing education for dentists. Let's start by developing a list of those who provide continuing education. Take a few minutes and think about who provides opportunities for continuing dental education. Let's make a list of those who provide these opportunities.
   LIST RESPONSES ON FLIP CHART
3. How do you find out about these opportunities?
   FOLLOW-UP:
   3A. If notices come by mail, does someone in your office screen these before you see them?
   3B. Have you given your staff instructions about screening your mail?

3C. What makes you read one piece of promotional mailing as opposed to another?

4. If you have a choice of several continuing education programs to choose from, what prompts you to register for one course over another?

    PROBES:

    Location

    Speaker

    Cost

    Sponsor

5. If you are in doubt about which course to take, what would you do in order to make the decision?

6. Think back to a continuing education course that you felt was particularly good. What made it so good?

7. Think back to a continuing education course that was disappointing to you. What made it disappointing?

8. When you hear of the university's continuing dental education program, what comes to mind?

    FOLLOW-UP:

    8A. How do the university's continuing education courses compare with others?

    8B. To what extent are these continuing education courses influenced by the image of the total university or the university school of dentistry?

9. Let's talk a bit about the topics of continuing education. At this point in your practice, what topics would be most beneficial to you. Take a moment and write down on a piece of paper several course topics that you would find helpful if offered by continuing education.

    AFTER A SHORT DELAY, SAY:

    Let's go around the table, and I will make a list of these topics.

    AFTER THE LIST HAS BEEN WRITTEN ON THE FLIP CHART, ASK:

    If you were to pick one of these as most important to you, which one would you select?

10. As you think about the next two to three years, what courses would be most helpful to you?

11. Suppose that *you* are in charge of continuing dental education for the university. Your job is to provide continuing courses that will be beneficial to practicing dentists and to do it in such a way that they would attend. What would you do? Let's go around the table and have each of you comment on this.

12. Our discussion tonight was to help us understand the educational needs of practicing dentists. Have we missed anything?

Statewide Needs and the Role of the University

1. Think for a moment about the day-to-day operations of your business. What is your greatest need?
2. Where do you see your business in the next three to five years?
3. What is the biggest obstacle in getting your business where you want it to be?
4. When you hear of (name of university), what comes to mind?
5. Think back over the past decade. In what ways has (name of university) helped you individually or helped your business?
6. How would you liked to be helped by (name of university)?
7. (Name of university) is unique in our state because it is the land-grant university in our state. As a land-grant university, it has several functions, including teaching, research, and service (or outreach). Let's talk about each of these functions. How could the university help you through its teaching?
8. How could the university help you through its research?
9. How could the university help you through its outreach or service?

   MAKE A LIST OF EACH OF THESE ON A FLIP CHART, AND WHEN FINISHED, ASK QUESTION 10.

10. Take a look at the items we've listed for teaching, research, and outreach. Which one item is most important to you?
11. What changes are necessary for you to get this help from the university?
12. In what ways might you be of assistance to (name of university)?
13. Our purpose today was to . . . (30-second description of purpose). Have we missed anything?
14. What to you has been the most important topic that we've discussed in the past two hours?

Local Business Needs Assessment

1. Through the media and local community contacts, we have become more aware that today's workforce is changing. What changes have you noticed within your own company or department?
2. What does your business do to provide ongoing training for your employees?
3. Based on what you are hearing from employees or supervisors, what kinds of knowledge, skills, and work habits do your employees need?
4. How is your business trying to address these needs at this time?

5. To what extent is there a gap between what training is needed and what is offered?
6. Community education provides educational opportunities that might be of benefit to your business. Here is a list of classes. Please put a check in front of those that would be of interest to you or your employees. Also, there is space at the bottom to add your own ideas or suggestions.
7. Under what circumstances would you send an employee to a community education course? Describe the person and the course.
8. What information would you need to know about potential courses and instructors to consider sending your employees to these classes?
9. For both employer and employee to be satisfied with a training session, what is needed?
10. How should we let you know about these courses?
11. In the two hours we've spent together today, of all the ideas you have heard, which one strikes you as the most relevant to your business?
12. Would you be interested in working with community education to pursue these ideas?

Nutrition Needs Assessment

Think about needs that relate to nutrition, food, and health.

1. What needs do you see? Let's make a list.
2. Who has these needs?
3. How many people have each need?
4. What is the severity of the need?
5. What are the consequences if the need isn't met?
6. What strengths or resources do we have that will address the need.
7. How will this change within the next three to five years?
8. What role should (name of agency) have in addressing these concerns?
9. What advice do you have for people in (name of agency) as they consider these needs?

Role of Spiritual Community in Youth Drug and Alcohol Prevention

1. What are the most serious problems facing young people in your community?
2. How do you see tobacco, alcohol, and drug use by young people in relation to the most serious problem you cited?

3. What factors do you think protect young people from using tobacco, alcohol, or other drugs?

4. In what ways does religion or spirituality protect young people?

   PROBES:

   How important are ceremonies or involvement in ritual for young people?

   How important is a strong inner sense of spirituality as a protecting factor?

   How important is regular attendance at services?

   How important is the practicing of religious beliefs?

5. When you get together with colleagues or friends in the spiritual community, how often does the topic of use of tobacco, alcohol, or other drugs by young people come up in conversation? And what is it that you talk about?

6. What do you feel is the proper role of religious organizations in preventing or responding to alcohol, tobacco, or other drug use problems by youth?

7. Has your congregation tried any specific strategies to influence or change the use of drugs by youth? If so, tell us about them.

8. Here's a list of things your organization might do.

   HAND OUT A LIST INCLUDING THE FOLLOWING ITEMS.

   Which of these would seem appropriate for your organization?

   - Sermon on drug use issues
   - Education for parents
   - Education for other adults
   - Support groups
   - Drug-free activities for youth

9. What might get in the way of your organization trying some of these strategies?

10. What help or support would you like to aid you in accomplishing any or some of the above?

11. Our purpose today was to find out more about how people in the spiritual community feel about the use of tobacco, alcohol, or other drugs by young people. Have we missed anything?

Role of Parents in Youth Drug and Alcohol Prevention

1. As you think about young people and the use of tobacco, alcohol, and other drugs, what are your concerns?

2. Which of these—tobacco, alcohol, or other drugs—is of greatest concern to you? Tell us why.

3. Is there a particular age group of youth that is of special concern to you?
4. What can parents say or do that would help prevent kids from using tobacco, alcohol, or other drugs?
5. Many of us have had experience talking to kids about tobacco, alcohol, or other drugs. Sometimes we feel those discussions go well, and sometimes they just don't. What works for you? What makes it go well? What doesn't work?
6. What can groups or agencies in your community do to prevent kids from having problems with tobacco, alcohol, or other drugs?
7. Parents have indicated a desire to have more support to prevent the use of tobacco, alcohol, or other drugs among kids. What help would you like to have available to you?
8. What changes would you like to see, if any, in media coverage of tobacco, alcohol, and other drugs?
   LISTEN FOR:
   > Newspapers
   > Television
   > Radio
   > Movies
   > Billboards
   > Ads

   PROBE IF NECESSARY
9. For this next question, we'll go around the table and ask everyone to respond. Suppose only one thing could be done in this area of tobacco, alcohol, or drug prevention. You could decide what it would be. What would you pick, and why?
10. Let me summarize the key points of our discussion. Does this summary sound complete?
11. Our purpose was to learn more about how parents in this community feel about teenage tobacco, alcohol, and drug use and to get some ideas of future action. Have we missed anything? Do you have any advice for us?

System Standards for K-12 Public Education

1. What school experience provided you with a lasting impression? Think back to an experience with school that was impressive to you, that made you proud, or that was disappointing to you. It could be as a student, a parent, a member of the community, or in another role.
2. What do you think are the purposes of school?
3. What do schools of the future need to be like to ensure the success of all learners? Describe these schools.

4. For a long time, we've determined school success by measuring those things that are relatively easy to count—attendance, classes, time in class, degrees held by teachers, or events attended by parents. Suppose, instead, that we measured success by what happens to the people—what they know or are able to do, or how they behave. What kinds of things should be measured?

5. Who needs to be involved to ensure the success of all learners? What should their role be?
   LISTEN FOR
       Teachers
       Support Staff
       Administrators
       Parents
       Students
       Community Members
   PROBE IF NECESSARY

6. Schools differ. Some are poor, some are average, and some are great. Think for a moment about those schools that are great. What words would you use to describe these great schools?
   MAKE A LIST OF WORDS ON A FLIP CHART.

7. What do we need to do to create schools like these great schools?

8. Do you have any suggestions for system standards?

9. Of all the topics that we've talked about today, what to you is the most important?

10. The purpose of our discussion was to identify standards that we can use to evaluate our schools. These standards will be used to help us improve the poor schools and recognize the great schools. What have we missed?

The Role of Higher Education in the Community

1. When you hear the words *higher education*, what comes to mind?

2. Name the institutions of higher education in our community, and describe how they are similar or different from each other.

3. Who are the customers of higher education? Pretend that you have four boxes, and into these boxes you need to place the customers of higher education. What would you call your boxes, and what categories of customers would you have?
   PAUSE AND WAIT FOR PARTICIPANTS TO COMPLETE THEIR BOXES. WHEN THEY ARE FINISHED, HAVE EACH PERSON HOLD UP HIS OR HER LIST OF CATEGORIES.

4. Which customer category is most important to you and for what reason?
5. I'd like you to participate in a short exercise.

Listed in the following two charts are words that might describe higher education in our community. Note that the words on the same line have opposite meanings. Place a checkmark (✓) in one of the seven spaces on each line to indicate how you feel about higher education in our community NOW. Then do the rating to show how you feel higher education in the community SHOULD BE in the future.

PAUSE AND WAIT FOR PARTICIPANTS TO FINISH.

Higher Education in Our Community Is Now							
Convenient							Inconvenient
Accessible							Inaccessible
Available							Unavailable
Expensive							Inexpensive
Fragmented							Coordinated
Responsive							Nonresponsive
Challenging							Not challenging
Practical							Impractical
Customer-focused							Not customer-focused
Exciting							Boring
Efficient							Inefficient
Future-oriented							Past-oriented
Cooperative							Competitive
High quality							Inferior quality
Streamlined							Bureaucratic
Personalized							Institutionalized
Interesting							Uninteresting
Concerned teachers							Indifferent teachers
Colleges work together							Colleges work independently

Higher Education in Our Community Should Be							
Convenient							Inconvenient
Accessible							Inaccessible
Available							Unavailable
Expensive							Inexpensive
Fragmented							Coordinated
Responsive							Nonresponsive
Challenging							Not challenging
Practical							Impractical
Customer-focused							Not customer-focused
Exciting							Boring
Efficient							Inefficient
Future-oriented							Past-oriented
Cooperative							Competitive
High quality							Inferior quality
Streamlined							Bureaucratic
Personalized							Institutionalized
Interesting							Uninteresting
Concerned teachers							Indifferent teachers
Colleges work together							Colleges work independently

6. Which set of words had the greatest gap between present and future? And which one is most important to you?
7. If you could redesign higher education in this community, what changes would you make?
8. As you think about higher education, what is most important to you personally?
9. Have you had any bad experiences with higher education in our community?
10. What has impressed you about higher education in our community?

Extension Agent Training Needs on Water Quality

1. What is the foremost concern about water quality in your county?
2. Water quality concerns change over time. What do you see as water quality concerns: in the past, at present, in the future?
3. How do you identify concerns that are important to spend time on?
4. Assume that concern about water quality stays at the status quo level in your county. What do you need to do your job as an extension agent?
5. What training do you need in water quality?
6. What one thing to you would make the training a success?
7. What one thing to you would make the training a failure?
8. Training can occur in many ways through various media. In Extension, we often use lectures and workshops, but other methods, such as correspondence, interactive television, or one-to-one contact, can be used as well. How would you prefer to receive training in water quality?
9. Who should provide that training?
10. What other organizations should be involved or should assist with the training?
    LISTEN FOR:
        Units/departments within the university
        Units/departments at the local, state, or federal levels
        Other
    PROBE IF NECESSARY
11. Who should participate in the training?
12. What final suggestions do you have for those who are planning the training?

Youth Focus Group on Tobacco, Alcohol, and Drug Prevention

1. What draws kids to tobacco, alcohol, or other drugs?
2. What helps young people stay away from tobacco, alcohol, or other drugs?
3. Which of these—tobacco, alcohol, or other drugs—is of greatest concern to you? Why?
4. Is there a particular group of youth that especially has problems with tobacco, alcohol, or other drugs?
5. What can adults say or do that would help prevent kids from using tobacco, alcohol, or other drugs?
6. What is the most effective way for adults to talk to you about tobacco, alcohol, or other drugs?

7. How about parents? What is the most effective way for parents to talk to you about tobacco, alcohol, or other drugs?

8. What can kids do to prevent other kids from having problems with tobacco, alcohol, or other drugs?

9. What can groups or agencies in your community do to prevent kids from having problems with tobacco, alcohol, or other drugs?

10. For this next question, we'll go around the table and ask everyone to respond. Suppose only one thing could be done to prevent the use of tobacco, alcohol, or other drugs by youth. You could decide what it would be. What would you pick and why?

11. Let me summarize the key points of our discussion.
    GIVE A BRIEF TWO-MINUTE SUMMARY.

    Does this summary sound complete? Do you have any revisions or additions?

Teen Pregnancy Prevention

1. Let's talk about classes where you've learned a lot. Think about these classes for a moment. What needs to happen for you to learn a lot in a class?

2. What's the most important thing a teacher can do to help students learn?

3. Let's talk about classes on sexuality. We're talking about any and all classes you've ever had in public schools that have talked about sex, including lessons as short as one period and as long as one year. Think about a time when you learned a great deal in a class on sexuality. Tell us about it.

4. What did the teacher do that helped you learn?
   LISTEN FOR:
   > Visuals
   > Role playing
   > Small group projects
   > Readings
   > Library assignments
   > Other
   PROBE IF NECESSARY

5. We're particularly interested in classes that help prevent teen pregnancy. Just how might a class help prevent pregnancy?

6. Tell me about classes you've had that you thought were particularly good at preventing pregnancy. What made them so good?

7. Suppose that you are the teacher of a class to prevent teen pregnancy. You want to be as successful as possible in this goal. What would you do?

8. How should a class on teen pregnancy prevention be taught differently if it includes teens of different races and cultures?

9. What role should parents play in classes on teen pregnancy prevention?

10. Our job is to find out how best to teach classes on teen pregnancy prevention in multicultural classrooms. Have we missed anything?

Teen Violence Prevention

1. Let's name some places where you feel safe and some places where you don't feel safe.
   MAKE LISTS ON A FLIP CHART.

2. What does the word *violence* mean to you? or
   What is your definition of violence?

3. Tell me about an example of violence you've witnessed or experienced in the community?*

4. What causes violence?
   LISTEN FOR:
   > Alcohol
   > Drugs
   > Bullying
   > Being Abused in the Past

   PROBE IF NECESSARY

5. Why are some people the victims or the targets of violence?

6. What can be done to avoid being a target of violence?

7. What can you do to help someone who is a victim of violence?

8. Some people cause violence. They are violent toward others. What can youth do to help those who initiate violence?

9. What can others do to stop violence?
   FOLLOW-UP
   9A. Parents
   9B. School personnel
   9C. Police and law enforcement
   9D. Others

10. If you could do one thing that would reduce violence in your community, what would it be?

11. What's the most important thing we talked about today?

---

*Be careful about these answers. If participants begin talking about personal family violence, you may need to remind them to keep the answers general. If you hear examples of abuse, you may be required to report them. Don't let this become a place for kids to swap scary stories of violence, but rather a forum to identify solution strategies. Celebrate the solutions, but don't emphasize the act of violence.

Violence Prevention and Treatment for a Category of People

1. Let's talk about violence. What is it, and when does it occur?
2. How about violence toward (name of category of person)? How or when does it occur?
3. How is violence toward (name of category) similar or different from violence toward other people?
4. What's needed to prevent violence toward (name of category)?
5. What's needed to help (name of category) who experience violence?
6. What are the barriers? What gets in the way of preventing violence?
7. What are barriers to treatment, the things that get in the way after someone has experienced violence?
8. What to you are the greatest barriers?
9. What's needed to overcome these barriers?
10. What traditions and strengths do (name of category) have that will help?
11. Is there anything we've missed?

Climate of Local High School

1. Take a piece of paper and write down three things you really like about your school. Let's make a list on the flip chart.
2. On the other side of the paper, write down three things that disappoint you about your school. Let's make a list.
3. Think back to an experience you had at school that was outstanding. Describe it.
   ENCOURAGE STORYTELLING.
4. If you were developing a report card for your school, what would be the important categories and what would be your grades?
5. What makes you proud of your school?
6. What do you like least about your school? What is disappointing to you?
7. If you could change one thing about your school, what would it be?
8. Think about all that we have talked about today. What do you think is most important?
9. Let me summarize the key points. Is this summary adequate?
10. Is there anything that we've missed?

Changing the Name of the Department

1. Think about the current name of the department. What do others say about the name of this department?
2. What are the positive aspects of the current name?
3. What are the negative aspects of the current name?
4. Two names have evolved from past discussions. They are Department of ABC and Department of XYZ. What would it take for either of these to be acceptable to you?
5. If you were deciding today on a new name for the department, what name would be your first choice, and for what reason?
6. What reservations do you have that you would like others to know about?
7. On the flip chart, I've made a list of the names that have been suggested. Use a seven-point scale and rate how much you like or dislike each choice.

Foundation Self-Assessment

1. Think about your experiences with foundations. What comes to mind when you think of foundations?
2. Based on your experiences, what do you see as the positive things foundations have done in your community?
3. Think about what foundations could do that might be less helpful to your community. What might happen that would hinder your community or produce less than desired results? What can be done to be sure that this doesn't happen?
4. Think about how foundations might hinder or make things worse in your community. What might happen that would actually make things worse? What can be done to be sure that this doesn't happen?
5. What things are still needed in your community? We are particularly interested in those situations where foundations could be most helpful in working with your community.
6. Currently, there is a lot of discussion about balancing between immediate needs of people and a longer-term strategy of addressing root causes. Foundations, like other nonprofits and government agencies, are wrestling with how to use scarce resources most efficiently. Where in this continuum do you see local foundations landing?
7. Where should foundation priorities be placed? (NOTE: PARTICIPANTS MIGHT ACTUALLY DISCUSS SOME OF THIS IN QUESTION 6.)

8. What long-term trends or issues in your community do you see on the horizon? What role do you see for foundations?
9. After a short break, several members from the foundation community will be joining us. I will present a short summary of our discussion, and each of you is welcome to add to that summary if you like. Before we break, I would like to go around the table and ask each of you what you feel is the most important thing that we should share with these foundation staff people.

Focus Group With Focus Group Moderators

1. What prompted you to get involved with focus groups?
2. Based on your experience, what are the major advantages and disadvantages of focus groups?
3. In what ways is the information obtained in a focus group different from that obtained using other methods, such as individual interviews, telephone interviews, or surveys?
4. What tips and advice do you have about:
   A. Multiple moderators
   B. In-house focus groups
   C. Telephone focus groups
   D. Special rooms with one-way mirrors
   E. Media focus groups
   F. Focus groups with sensitive topics
   G. Focus groups with youth
   H. Focus groups with communities of color
5. What analysis strategies have you found helpful?
6. As you reflect on what has been written about focus groups, what gaps do you see?
7. What's the future of focus groups?

Testing the Proposal for a New Educational Effort

1. What's your first impression of the idea?
2. What are the advantages or positive aspects of the proposal?
3. What are the disadvantages or negative aspects of the proposal?
4. For the learning center to be successful, what must happen?
5. What are the next steps that we should take?

Pilot Testing New Materials

1. Take a few moments and look over the materials. They include a brief description of a program and examples of handouts that participants would get.

2. What one thing do you like the best?
3. What one thing do you like the least?
4. If you could change one thing about the materials, what would it be?
5. What would get you to participate in this program?
6. Suppose that you were trying to encourage a friend to participate in this program. What would you say?
7. Do you have any other advice for us as we introduce this new program?

Formative Program Evaluation

1. Tell us how you participated in the program.
2. What did you like best about the program? (What has been most helpful to you?)
3. What did you like the least about the program? (What was least helpful to you?)
4. What should be changed?
5. What should be continued just as it is now?
6. What should be continued but fine tuned?
7. What should be dropped?
8. Do you have any other advice about the program?

Complaint System Questions

1. Can you remember a time when you were very pleased with a product or service? It could have been at a restaurant or a store, and you felt good about what happened. Tell us about it.
2. Think about the last time you complained about a product or service. Tell us what happened.
3. Have you ever thought about complaining but decided not to say anything? Tell us about it.
4. Think about service complaints in any governmental organization and in the private sector. Are complaints handled differently?
5. Think about your experiences with (name of agency). Have you ever complained or thought about making a complaint? Tell us about it.
6. Has anyone ever complained to you about some service or product you provided? What did you do about the complaint?
7. For this next question, you'll need this piece of paper. Pretend that we're putting together a report card for (name of agency). Think about the categories of complaints. What

categories would be needed for the report card? Write the possible categories on the paper.

WAIT A FEW MINUTES FOR PARTICIPANTS TO COMPLETE THEIR LISTS.

OK, let's list your categories on the flip chart.

8. How do we encourage people or make them feel it's all right to give us feedback or to make complaints?
9. When we receive a complaint, what should be done about it?
10. What does "resolving" a complaint mean to you?
11. Think about all that we have talked about today. What do you think is most important for (name of agency) to keep doing?
12. Was the summary adequate? Have we missed anything?

Community Assessment

1. The word *community* can mean a number of things. Describe your community. Who is in it? What is it like? What are its key values?
2. What are the strengths of your community?
3. How has your community changed in the past five years?
4. If someone from outside the community wanted to find out what the specific needs and assets of the community are, how would this be done? Who would be listened to? What should be looked at?
5. What traditions of giving or sharing exist within your community? (How do people help each other in your community?)
6. How about cooperation? In what ways does your community work together?
7. What are the obstacles or barriers to working together?
8. In what ways does your community work with other communities?
9. When you hear of the (name of community foundation), what comes to mind?
   PASS AROUND THE HANDOUT.
10. Think about how (name of foundation) might benefit your community. Specifically, think about things other than money. What comes to mind?
11. Think about how (name of foundation) might hinder or make things worse in your community. What might happen that would actually make things worse?
12. Our purpose in this discussion was to find out how (name of foundation) can better serve your community and people. This could occur in a variety of ways. It might mean

providing people in your community with skills, expertise, money, or other forms of support. Think about what we've talked about. Have we missed anything?

Inventory of Church Members

1. What prompted you to join (name of church)?
2. What do you expect of a church in your life?
3. To what extent has (name of church) fulfilled your expectations?

   PAUSE AND WAIT FOR RESPONSES.

   LISTEN FOR:
   > Worship Service
   > Music
   > Sermons
   > Communion
   > Participation by Lay Members
   > Special events
   > Contemporary Services

   PROBE IF NECESSARY
4. (Name of church) has a three-pronged approach to programming. It consists of worship, education, and outreach. Let's talk about the outreach effort. What's working well? What's not working well?
5. People in crises seek support from others who might be in similar situations. What kinds of support do you feel should be available through our church?
6. In a congregation the size of (name of church), it is hard to keep everyone informed. What suggestions do you have to increase our feeling of unity?
7. What would you like to see happen in (name of church) that would really turn you on?
8. If you were to make one improvement in the church, what would it be?
9. What can *you* do to improve (name of church)?
10. I'd like to summarize our conversation.

    GIVE SUMMARY.

    Is this summary complete?

Summary and Thank You

Closing prayer

References

Branthwaite, A., & Lunn, T. (1985). Projective techniques in social and market research. In R. Walker (Ed.), *Applied qualitative research* (pp. 101-121). London: Gower.

Chesterton, G. K. (1951). The invisible man. In *The Father Brown Omnibus,* p. 58. New York: Dodd, Mead.

Glaser, B. G., & Strauss, A. L. *The discovery of grounded theory.* New York: Aldine de Gruyter.

Henderson, N. R. (1994, December). Asking effective focus group questions, *Quirk's Marketing Research Review,* 8(10), especially pp. 8-9, 34-35.

Lazarfeld, P. (1986). *The art of asking why.* New York: The Advertising Research Foundation. (Original work published in 1934 in *The National Marketing Review*)

Index to This Volume

Index to the Focus Group Kit

The letter preceding the page number refers to the volume, according to the following key:

About the Author

Richard A. Krueger is a professor and evaluation leader at the University of Minnesota. He teaches in the College of Education and Human Development and serves as an evaluation specialist with the University of Minnesota Extension Service. Over the past decade, he has taught hundreds of people to plan, conduct, and analyze focus group interviews. He loves stories. Perhaps that is what drew him to focus group interviews.  Where else can one hear so many stories in such a short period of time?